Ni'n na L'nu

the Mi'kmaq of Prince Edward Island

by A.J.B. Johnston and Jesse Francis

ACORNPRESS

Charlottetown
2013

Ni'n na L'nu : the Mi'kmaq of Prince Edward Island

Text © 2013 by Jesse Francis and A. J. B. Johnston
ISBN 978-1-894838-93-1

Designed by Stéphane Breton
Editing by Jane Ledwall
Printed in Canada by Friesens

The publisher acknowledges the support of the Government
of Canada through the Canada Book Fund of the Department
of Canadian Heritage for our publishing activities. We also
acknowledge the support of the Canada Council for the Arts
for our publishing program.

Canada Council   Conseil des arts
for the Arts   du Canada

Canadian   Patrimoine
Heritage   canadien

Library and Archives Canada Cataloguing in Publication

Johnston, A. J. B., author
Ni'n na L'nu : the Mi'kmaq of Prince Edward Island / A.J.B Johnston
and Jesse Francis.

This is a companion volume to the travelling exhibition
of the same name held at the Confederation Centre in
Charlottetown in August 2013.
ISBN 978-1-894838-93-1 (pbk.)

1. Micmac Indians—Prince Edward Island—History.
2. Micmac Indians—Prince Edward Island—History—Pictorial works.
I. Johnston, A. J. B, author
II. Title.

E99.M6J64 2013   971.7004'97343   C2013-904590-2

Foreword

Chief Matilda Ramjattan,
Lennox Island First Nation,
Co-Chair, Mi'kmaq
Confederacy of PEI

Chief Brian Francis,
Abegweit First Nation,
Co-Chair, Mi'kmaq
Confederacy of PEI

As proud Mi'kmaq from Prince Edward Island, we were fortunate to grow up with a connection to our heritage. We know our family histories, and we still feel a deep connection to the land. In recent decades, our awareness of the ancient people from which we descend has only been enhanced, especially by archaeological findings on the Island. That research, along with oral history projects that record the knowledge of the Elders, has greatly improved our knowledge of the many traditions we are fortunate to inherit. It is our responsibility to pass on that knowledge and appreciation to the generations to come.

Although it was not that long ago, the era in which we grew up was quite different from that which our youth experience today. The world is changing rapidly, especially in terms of technology. For many Mi'kmaw youth it's hard to grasp their ancestors' ways of life of even a few generations ago. And yet, it is too rich a heritage to lose. We must do all we can so our young people continue to feel the connections with the ancient traditions and with this land.

Likewise, for many non-Aboriginal Islanders, the Mi'kmaw heritage of our Island home (Epekwitk) is not as widely or well-known as it deserves. As for those who are not from Prince Edward Island, in some cases they are completely unaware that there has for millennia been a continuous, vital Aboriginal presence here.

This book and the travelling exhibition that it accompanies bring a wide-ranging look at the Mi'kmaq of Epekwitk: from the landscape that sustained our ancient forebears, to the effects of European wars in Mi'kmaw territory; from the Mi'kmaw lifestyles that allowed our people to survive, to our contribution to the World Wars; and, throughout, to an appreciation of Mi'kmaw poetry, arts, craft, music, and much more.

The Mi'kmaq Confederacy of Prince Edward Island serves as the common voice for the Mi'kmaw governments of PEI and provides services to its communities in a wide variety of areas, including education, health, culture and heritage, and justice. We are proud of our sponsorship of this book and the companion exhibition. We believe they make a valuable and lasting contribution to the understanding of our proud history and vibrant culture.

Over the past number of years, Parks Canada and the Mi'kmaq Confederacy have forged a close working relationship. Since 2005, our organizations have co-funded a Joint Projects Manager position to work toward accomplishing mutual goals. This book and the travelling exhibition have benefited in various ways from that partnership and the cooperative spirit of our work.

We hope you find this book enlightening and enjoyable.

Chief Matilda Ramjattan
Chief Brian Francis

for Moira and for Hannah and Colin

Table of Contents

Introduction

It's no easy matter to write a book about the Mi'kmaq of what today is called Prince Edward Island. The people at the centre of the story have experienced and accomplished so much and over such an incredibly long time. The first questions any author has to ask are: Where should I begin such a story? What do I possibly include, and what regrettably do I leave out? In the case of this book, the author is not singular but plural. There are two of us, and neither is of Mi'kmaw descent. For us, as for anyone else wishing to write a similar book, there are no easy answers to the questions above. Yet over time we made our choices, and those choices constitute this book.

This text is a companion to a travelling exhibition of the same name. That exhibition was a project envisioned by the Mi'kmaq Confederacy of Prince Edward Island. Working with the Mi'kmaq Confederacy and an advisory group of Mi'kmaq and non-Aboriginal specialists, Camus Productions Inc. conceived, designed, and oversaw the fabrication of the exhibition. The two authors of this book were involved in that process every step of the way: A.J.B. (John) Johnston was the lead researcher and writer of the travelling exhibition; Jesse Francis managed the creation of that exhibition for the Mi'kmaq Confederacy. Along the journey, the idea of a companion book emerged. It seemed like a good idea, a natural outgrowth of the exhibition.

Though a Nova Scotia scene painted by H.N. Binney in the 1790s, this could easily have been Prince Edward Island Mi'kmaq of the time.

Happily, The Acorn Press, the Island's renowned publisher, agreed. The Mi'kmaq Confederacy provided valuable resources and sponsorship. So *Ni'n na L'nu* now takes two forms: a travelling exhibition and this book.

Neither author wanted the book simply to be a catalogue of the exhibition. We both thought it should take the content of the exhibit and give it a different life. While the book does cover much of the same ground and reproduces many of the images found on the five stylized wigwams of the exhibition, there is much additional written and visual material as well. The book also has a different tone and voice. While we might hope every reader of this book will enjoy the exhibition, and every viewer of the exhibit will read the book, we realize that will not be the case.

So, where should this particular story of the Mi'kmaq begin? Most books about the history of this or that people or place in North America begin with an arrival or a founding. Or sometimes with the background context that led to that arrival or founding. Obviously, with the Mi'kmaq as with any of the First Peoples in Canada, that model is not going to work. We're not talking about a timeline of a few centuries but millennia. Not as long as geological time to be sure, but the telling of the Mi'kmaw story is nonetheless quite different than the telling of the story of any European or other people who crossed the Atlantic two or four centuries ago.

Micmac, Mi'kmaq, Mi'kmaw, or Migmag?

The answer to that question is not as simple as one might hope or expect. That's because there are several different orthographies for the language of the Mi'kmaq. The one used most commonly in Prince Edward Island and throughout Nova Scotia differs from an earlier orthography still used in parts of New Brunswick and in Quebec. And to further complicate matters, the spelling of the term varies for the singular or plural name for the people and for using the term as an adjective or a noun.

In this book, when we use the terms Mi'kmaq and Mi'kmaw, we are following the Smith-Francis orthography. In that approach to the ancient language, Mi'kmaq is the spelling of the word for the people overall. Mi'kmaw refers to a single individual and is also the adjectival form. Thus, you could have a sentence that reads: The Mi'kmaq speak the Mi'kmaw language.

The Mi'kmaq of Nova Scotia have been using the Smith-Francis orthography for about thirty years. The switch to that same system of spelling came later on Prince Edward Island, and there is now a concerted effort among Mi'kmaw people to standardize orthography. The Mi'kmaq Confederacy of PEI officially adopted the Smith-Francis system in 2008.

So why is the "Mi'kmaq Confederacy of PEI" spelled as it is when according to Smith-Francis it should be the "Mi'kmaw Confederacy"? The word Mi'kmaq was used widely on the Island when the M'ikmaq Confederacy of PEI was formed. However, the adjectival form "Mi'kmaw" was not adopted into common usage so quickly on Prince Edward Island. So "Mi'kmaq Confederacy" became the registered legal name for the organization, and it remains so.

Even in more recent times, during what is known as the colonial era and the more modern period that came after, the mainstream groups of society often considered the Mi'kmaq of marginal interest, or worse, a people destined to disappear. Among the many implications of such an attitude, one outcome was that few images or documents were generated to tell the people's story. Yet "few" is not none. Through the companion exhibition and this book, a wealth of family photos and little known older images speak to us across the span of time.

As for the other big questions of what to cover and what to leave out, we decided early on to narrow the field of inquiry to five broad themes. Those themes are the chapters of this book and the subjects of the exhibition's five stylized wigwams. We do not pretend to tell everything about the Mi'kmaq of PEI, because that would be impossible. Yet, we believe there is enough here to keep any reader interested and absorbed for an hour or two. Maybe this combination of texts and images will encourage you to seek out and explore the special Mi'kmaw landscapes of Prince Edward Island. Or even better, to discuss history and life's lived experiences with a Mi'kmaw Elder. However, if such an education is not immediately available to you, this book might perhaps be seen as a temporary and partial substitute.

A final word: our hope in putting together this book was not to define or deconstruct the Mi'kmaq. These pages are not a homework assignment or any kind of medicine one should take. On the contrary, we believe that the story of the Island's Mi'kmaq is fascinating and important in itself and that when it is fairly told it stands as the equal to any other people's history. If we had to select a pithy description of what we want our book to accomplish, it might be this: We want to share with everyone what we ourselves have learned. We hope you enjoy the book.

"Big" Isaac Peters and and Denny Lewis, around 1920.
Photo courtesy Vincent Tuplin.

Madeline Thomas and her daughter, 1930s.
Photo courtesy Vincent Tuplin.

In 1911, Thomas became the first Islander to run the Boston Marathon. He placed twenty-sixth in a field of 127. The field in 1911 was strong and Michael's time was actually better than that of the race winners in 1909 and 1910. It is also notable that due to an accident involving his support cyclist, he ran the race without water or refreshments.

The early twentieth century saw long-distance running become an important spectator sport. Champion long-distance runners were well known and widely popular. The reception and parade for Thomas held in Charlottetown following his Halifax win in 1910 was the largest athletic celebration in the history of the city at the time.

MICHAEL THOMAS, 1885–1954

Michael Thomas was born on Lennox Island. Though inclined to athletics, "Mick" was in his mid-twenties before Fr. John A. MacDonald, the local priest, encouraged him to take up running seriously and competitively. Michael went on to numerous notable wins in races around eastern Canada. He placed first in the Charlottetown Patriot Ten-Mile, in 1909, 1910, and 1911, and won the *Halifax Herald–Mail* Ten-Mile Road Race, considered the most prestigious in eastern Canada, in 1910, 1911, and 1912. The Halifax race at the time attracted large, highly competitive fields, including the top North American distance runners.

Michael Thomas's non-athletic accomplishments are as notable his athletic ones. Thomas's daughter Lillian Haroulakis describes him:

To me, Michael Thomas was above all my Dad: a kind, gentle, and understanding father. I was close to him; we often went fishing together. While on Lennox Island, prior to our move to Stratford, he and my mother Mary Anne provided for our family through mixed farming and fishing. We lived comfortably in our Mi'kmaq community. However, job opportunities and especially educational opportunities for their six girls made them decide to move us to what is now Stratford. The move wasn't an easy one but proved to be a good decision; my father worked fishing from Southport, and my sisters and I received our education from the Sisters at St. Joseph's Convent. My father was very encouraging of us; four girls went on to commercial college and two joined the Armed Forces, serving with the CAWC.

My father was a humble man who seldom spoke about his running. I learned about his achievements as a runner from other people and from old newspaper clippings.

Life for Michael and his family was not without hardship or tragedy. In 1952 his beloved wife Mary Anne and their granddaughter were lost in a fire that destroyed their home. Lillian writes, "My father earned some fame as a runner but he earned little money. He ran because he loved to do it. He was good at it.

My father was an outstanding role model; someone who was proud of his community and made his community proud. He was a proud Mi'kmaq, an accomplished athlete, a fisherman, a good neighbour, a good husband and a kind and loving father." Michael Thomas is warmly remembered as a fine athlete and a fine human being.

Michael Thomas and his wife Mary Anne.

Our home is this country
Across windswept hills
With snow on fields
The cold air.

I like to think of our native life,
Curious, free,
And look at the stars
Sending icy messages.
My eyes see the cold face of the moon
Cast his net over the bay.

It seems
We are like the moon—
Born,
Grow slowly,
Then fade away, to reappear again
In a never-ending cycle.

Our lives go on
Until we are old and wise.
Then end.

We are no more,
Except we leave
A heritage that never dies.

—Rita Joe, Mi'kmaw poet

Since Before Long Ago
Kesi-sa'q a

Where exactly do we begin the story of the Mi'kmaq of *Epekwitk*? First, we recommend dropping the word "exactly" from the question. The history of the Mi'kmaq, like the history of all Aboriginal peoples of the Americas, goes back so long that it does not lend itself to a retelling of events as a parade of particular dates. The chapter title's four words, "Since Before Long Ago," are deliberately imprecise, and more powerful and more truthful for that. With the Mi'kmaq, we are not talking of a history of a mere four or five hundred years. We're talking millennia. And when one starts thinking in millennia, it is difficult to grasp the span of time.

The evidence from the ancient time is not found in archives. It's found in and on the land—as in archaeological sites—and in stories, in the oral traditions and values of a people whose connections go back farther than recorded time. This chapter will present some important dates but will also go back farther, through the evidence in the land and the stories, to explore the origins of Mi'kmaw tradition and territory.

Despite our comments above about not wanting to (or not being able to) focus on a cavalcade of dates, it is important to acknowledge events of importance to the Mi'kmaq that *did* occur on specific dates within the relatively recent past and particularly from the 1600s onward. Various arrivals and departures and wars and treaties within the past few centuries had great effects on the Island's Aboriginal people for better or (more often) for worse. However, the past few centuries of interaction between the Mi'kmaq and the newcomer colonial peoples and regimes represent but a fraction of the total era the Mi'kmaq have been on the island now called Prince Edward Island. In reality, the ancestors of today's Mi'kmaq have been on the Island since before there even was an island at all.

Epekwitk = PEI

Epekwitk has been the Mi'kmaw name for what is now known to most people as Prince Edward Island for a very long time. Prior to the introduction of the Smith-Francis orthography, Epekwitk was most often spelled in an anglicized form as Abegweit. It's the same word and idea; only the spelling has changed. In the language of the Mi'kmaq, the word means "lying in the water," which is precisely what the island does. Prior to calling the Island Epekwitk, the Mi'kmaq knew this part of the world as Kjiktu'lnu, which meant "our great boat." Beginning in the 1500s, French mariners gave the island a new name; they called it Île Saint-Jean. After the British captured Louisbourg in 1758 they were given Île Saint-Jean as part of the surrender document. The British translated the name and the island became St. John's Island. That lasted until 1799. Confusion over which St. John was which—there were others in New Brunswick, Newfoundland, the Caribbean, and the Pacific—led the British authorities to give it a new name, one it has to this day: Prince Edward Island. The choice was to honour Prince Edward, Duke of Kent. It is important to recall, however, the names of Kjiktu'lnu and Epekwitk.

While envisioning Mi'kmaw history as a straight timeline unfolding along a series of pinned-down dates is not going to work, the idea of timeline per se is not bad.

Mi'kmaw woman's peaked hat, from the collection of the Prince Edward Island Museum and Heritage Foundation. Photo: John Sylvester, copyright Mi'kmaq Confederacy of PEI.

We imagine a timeline for the Mi'kmaq that has many twists: so many that it becomes a spiral. A spiral is perhaps the best image for picturing time not as something linear, relentlessly marching forward—which is how Europeans and people of European descent have largely viewed history for a few hundred years—but rather as something curved and expanding. Such an approach, we have learned from talking with Elders, is perhaps closer to how people—not just the Mi'kmaq but everyone—really live their lives. A spiral better reflects the repetition and cycles of life and nature and also the changing and forward motion of time.

Mi'kmaw history and culture are inseparable from the natural world that nurtured and sustained The People. And nature abounds in cycles. We see it every time the sun sets at night and reappears the next morning. Or when winter moves into spring and on to summer and then autumn before repeating the sequence one more time. Or when the tides rise and fall twice a day according to the phases of the moon. Or in the myriad examples of life cycles for every species that lives, matures, and dies, which is every single one. All of us upon this planet are subject to natural forces greater than we control. And those forces move in cycles. Which brings us back to what the Elders suggest, that we begin to see the history of the Mi'kmaq not as a linear unfolding but as a gently curving shape.

The curve of a spiral Mi'kmaw timeline begins about 12,000 years ago, when the people considered the ancient ancestors of the Mi'kmaq came to live on the land that is now Prince Edward Island. It is not possible, nor is there any need, to be more precise than that.

Archaeologists describe the first inhabitants of the Maritimes as Palaeo-Indians. "Palaeo-Indian" isn't really an identifier for a people but rather for a time period and for the kinds of stone tools the people used back then and left behind to be found. In the view of the Mi'kmaq there is a continuous evolution of their ancestors from the Palaeo era through the spiral of time to today. The terms they use for those ancestors and the dates of their living time are as follows:

13,500 before present (BP): Ancient People, Sa'qewe'k L'nu'k (Palaeo Period)

10,000–3,000 BP: Not So Recent People, Mu Awsami Kejikawe'k L'nu'k (Archaic Period)

3,000–500 BP: Recent People, Kejikawe'k L'nu'k (Woodland to Early Contact Period)

500 BP–Present: Today's People, Kiskuke'k L'nu'k (European Contact)

Geologists and climatologists tell us the evidence shows that 12,000 years ago, the last Ice Age was ending. All the water in those vast receding ice sheets had come from the sea. That meant that in the last Ice Age, sea level in the Maritimes was approximately 65 metres (213.25 feet) below where it stands today. It takes one's breath away to imagine the relationship of landscape and seascape back then. The climate was not only much cooler and more tundra-like, but the coastlines were nowhere near where they now are. Halifax's Bedford Basin, for instance, was still an inland lake. The sliver of sand dune off Nova Scotia's eastern shore now known as Sable Island was then a vast tract of land.

And, most important of all from the perspective of Prince Edward Islanders, there was no Prince Edward Island. We're not speaking of the name, "Prince Edward Island," which was given to the Island in 1799, but the fact of islandness, of being surrounded by the sea. That land that is now PEI did not become an island by definition until between 5,000 and 7,000 years ago, when the combined effect of melting glaciers and crustal subsidence (the gradual downward settling of the earth's surface with little or no horizontal motion) created the Northumberland Strait. Over time, what began as a relatively shallow body of water has grown steadily deeper and kept Epekwitk separated from the mainland of Canada.

Prior to that, however, for several thousand years, the long-ago Mi'kmaq could walk from what is now called Wood Islands, Prince Edward Island, to Caribou, Nova Scotia, where the passenger ferry runs today, or from and to many other locations along what now are two separated shores. Today, one of the Mi'kmaw districts, Epekwitk aq Piktuk, or PEI and the Pictou shores, links two shores together in a single district. This allows us to speculate that the district's origins date back to before the sea rose up to create the Northumberland Strait. If so, then the route the ancestors once walked across by land, centuries and millennia later the Mi'kmaq traversed in their sea-going canoes.

Winter Travel, a painting by Mi'kmaw artist Roger Simon. Reproduced with the permission of Vienna Sanipass and Metepnagiag Heritage Park.

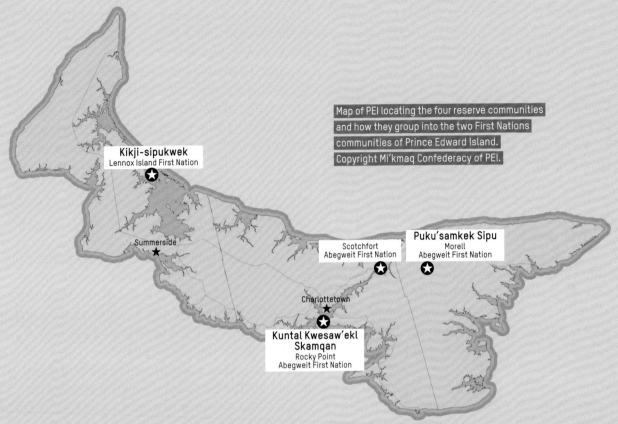

Kikji-sipukwek
Lennox Island First Nation

Summerside

Map of PEI locating the four reserve communities and how they group into the two First Nations communities of Prince Edward Island. Copyright Mi'kmaq Confederacy of PEI.

Puku'samkek Sipu
Morell
Abegweit First Nation

Scotchfort
Abegweit First Nation

Charlottetown

Kuntal Kwesaw'ekl
Skamqan
Rocky Point
Abegweit First Nation

The Big Picture

In round figures there are about forty thousand Mi'kmaq in the entire world. Most live within the same region that formed the traditional territories of their ancestors, along the eastern seaboard of North America. There are thirty-one Mi'kmaw First Nations or "bands" in Atlantic Canada and one in the state of Maine. On Prince Edward Island the First Nations are those of Lennox Island and Abegweit. Some First Nations are comprised of several geographically distinct communities. For example, the Abegweit First Nation is made up of the communities of Scotchfort, Rocky Point, and Morell.

The Mi'kmaw language is no longer spoken by every person of Mi'kmaw descent. Instead, English is the dominant tongue, although French is spoken by some Mi'kmaq in Quebec. In some Mi'kmaw communities such as Eskasoni in Cape Breton and Elsipogtog in New Brunswick, the Mi'kmaw language has remained relatively strong. In others, especially the smaller communities, it has fared less well. In some areas it has nearly disappeared. Of late, however, new language programs are helping spoken and written Mi'kmaq make a comeback everywhere.

It's important to bear in mind that the earliest Aboriginal population was living in an ecosystem unlike anything we know today. It was a largely tundra-like landscape. The people lived in small groups organized around extended families, and they moved on a seasonal basis to obtain their food and everything else they needed for sustenance. In some parts of the world people still live that way. In fact, go back far enough in time, and that's how everyone's ancestors once lived.

In the case of the Mi'kmaq in the ancestral era, their seasonal round involved not only hunting animals of all kinds (of the land, sea, and air), but also harvesting the bounty of the plant world. From animals came food to eat, hides and pelts to turn into clothing, and bones, horns, and shells to adapt into tools or to use as ornamentation. From plants and trees came medicines, dyes, tobacco, wood, bark, and roots to sew bark. Then there were stones. Some could be shaped into tools; others provided mineral pigments to use as dyes.

Portability was essential to the migratory lifestyle, and the people used great ingenuity to create shelters from the elements. In the winter, they moved inland to where they could hunt and trap mammals large and small. In the warmer months they harvested fish, shellfish, birds, bird eggs, and mammals such as seals and walrus on the coast and out to sea. Compared to the present, that coast was generally farther out than it is now (and much further out the further back in time one goes). Evidence of the weapons or tools those early people used occasionally surfaces in a fishing net. There have been finds dragged or trawled up from what today is covered by water.

Because of rising sea levels and the advance of the sea over millennia, many early coastal sites of Aboriginal people are unavailable for protection or research. For example, what is known to archaeologists as the Jones site is now located on the shores of St. Peters Bay, only a few hundred metres from Prince Edward Island's north shore and the Gulf of St. Lawrence. However, during the earliest period of habitation there, that same site was along the shores of a river, and many kilometres from the sea. There is no radio-carbon dating for the Jones site, but it is thought to represent the late Palaeo or early Archaic period.

Moving off PEI to high-ground sites in nearby Nova Scotia, archaeologists have done extensive work in the Debert-Belmont area. The initial excavations were in the 1960s, and there has been more work done there since. The ancestors of the Mi'kmaq were living in that part of what is now Nova Scotia about 13,500 years ago. Presumably, they were also living in other locations around the Maritimes at the same time or not long after; it's just that evidence has not survived or not yet been uncovered. The Confederacy of Mainland Mi'kmaq is developing exciting plans to create a museum and exhibit centre called Mi'kmawey Debert to highlight what has been learned about the Debert-Belmont Palaeo site.

13 000 BP

The landscape beneath the glaciers about 13,000 years before present. Image: John Shaw, NRCAN.

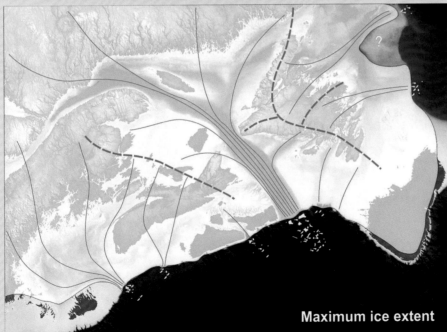

Maximum ice extent

The maximum extent of glaciations long ago. Image: John Shaw, NRCAN.

Digging Down with Science,
Menaqa Ankaprmik Saynsiktuk

Over the past few decades the Mi'kmaq of Prince Edward Island have worked with professional archaeologists to recover knowledge of times long ago. Using the latest technology and excavating with a scientific focus, a skilled archaeologist can go back in time. The ancestors of the Mi'kmaq had left many traces of their presence on *Epekwitk* all across the Island. One of the best-known of the archaeological sites is the Jones Site on the Greenwich Peninsula on the shores of St. Peters Bay. The site was named after Roland Jones, the amateur archaeologist who discovered it in the 1960s. The site is now preserved in the Greenwich area of Prince Edward Island National Park. The objects uncovered at the Jones Site date back to as long ago as 9,000 and 10,000 years before present and up to the period of early European settlement. This suggests an almost continuous use of the site over thousands of years.

The MCPEI is partnering with the Aboriginal Affairs Secretariat of the Government of Prince Edward Island to assist with ongoing work at various Island archaeological sites, such as at Pitawelkek on Hog Island in Malpeque Bay.

When archaeological analysis is combined with the stories and knowledge of the Elders, it helps shed even more light on ancient times of the Mi'kmaq.

Typical stone tools found at Prince Edward Island archaeological sites. Photos: John Sylvester, copyright Mi'kmaq Confederacy of PEI.

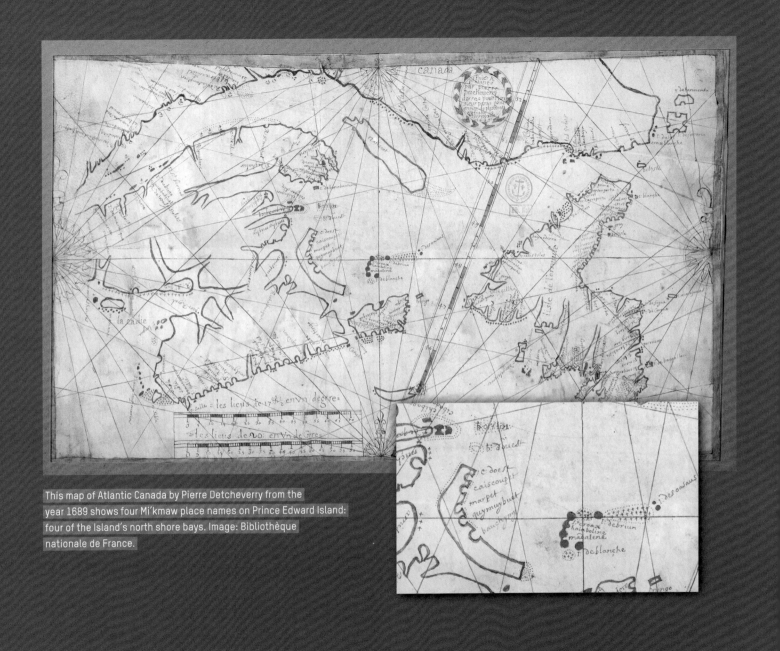

This map of Atlantic Canada by Pierre Detcheverry from the year 1689 shows four Mi'kmaw place names on Prince Edward Island: four of the Island's north shore bays. Image: Bibliothèque nationale de France.

As the last Ice Age ended, the ice did not melt overnight. At its peak, that ice was up to two kilometres thick. The melting took many centuries before the ice was completely gone. And, in fact, the warming era was not continuous. There were times, sometimes decades and sometimes centuries, in which cold weather returned. For long periods, the glaciers either did not melt or began to grow again. The ancient ancestors of the Mi'kmaq had to adapt to whatever climate change came their way. This begins to explain the profound connection the Mi'kmaq have to the land. It has nourished them since time immemorial, over thousands of years during which the land and sea relationship and the living conditions of the creatures (land animals, fish, and birds) were constantly altering.

A variety of artifacts from Prince Edward Island sites. The smallest point is of unknown origin. Photo: John Sylvester, copyright Mi'kmaq Confederacy of PEI.

The Jones site excavation under way in 1985, led by Dr. David Keenlyside, of the Canadian Museum of Civilization. Photo: David Keenlyside, Canadian Museum of Civilization.

Since long ago, the Mi'kmaq have referred to themselves as "the people," as epitomized in the phrase *Ni'n na L'nu* ("I am one of the people"). So where does the word Mi'kmaq come from? It's a variation on an ancient word in their language, *nikmaq*. It was a common greeting and meant roughly "my family," "my connections," and "my kin." It really describes a family relationship among people, not the people themselves. In the time of earliest contact between Europeans and the ancestors of today's Mi'kmaq, the Europeans did not understand the language they were hearing the Mi'kmaq speak, nor the complexity of Mi'kmaw society. They often made judgments based on fleeting and incidental encounters. One word the Europeans apparently heard a lot from the Mi'kmaq, spoken as a greeting, was *nikmaq*. Over time, the "n" sound became an "m" sound, and the word became "Micmac" (with various spellings). It became the word the French used to describe *L'nuk*, or the people. The designation stuck.

"In a Natural State"

The French and Acadians ended up having much closer relations with the Mi'kmaq of *Epekwitk* (and elsewhere in the Maritimes) than the British colonists generally did. In the French language of the colonial era, a term often used to describe the Aboriginal peoples of the Americas was *sauvages*. The word has a long history of being erroneously translated into English as "savages." In truth, in French, the word denoted a people "living in a natural state." The term was used to distinguish the Mi'kmaq and other indigenous peoples from the Europeans. That is, the newly encountered peoples of the Americas dressed and lived much differently than did the Europeans, closer to what the French regarded as a natural state, or *sauvage*. The use of the term did not signify ferocity or a threat such as the word "savage" does in English. The mistranslation of the French word lasted for centuries, with serious negative consequences for many generations of Aboriginal people.

"L'nu" means "one person."
"L'nuk" means "many people."

Prior to that term predominating, the earliest European explorers and missionaries came up with other names for the Mi'kmaq. The three most common early terms were *Gaspésiens, Souriquois,* and *Tarrantines*. The first of those names meant "of or from the Gaspé," which was (and still is) a district of the Mi'kmaq. The second name comes from a Basque word and makes a reference to the Suricoa River. The third designation, *Tarrantines*, came from a sixteenth-century English poem about a mythical land called Arcadia. None of those names lived on to the 1700s. Some Europeans of course preferred the broad generic "Indians," as was used across the Americas. The fact that it was based on a mistaken geographical belief that the Europeans had arrived in southeast Asia (India) does not seem to have bothered those who used the name.

Essential to every human community are the stories we tell. Narratives are a defining characteristic of our human species; they are what make us—as individuals and as groups—who we are. So it is and always has been with the Mi'kmaq. Their storytelling traditions go back thousands of years. It is not possible to overstate how important those tales and legends have been. In traditional times they were not simply pastimes or entertainment told at firesides or inside wigwams or while travelling from place to place. On the contrary, the living ancient tales—living because they would at each telling be infused with the personality of the teller and could be refined with improvisations as they were passed on and retold—served many practical purposes.

The stories subtly made points about what a person's moral code should be. They suggested how people should (and should not) interact with each other. They addressed spiritual and holistic matters by pointing out how the actors in the tales were part of a living, changing environment of land, lake, river, and sea. The stories told that animals, birds, and fish were all part of that world, as equal partners; people could sometimes move back and forth from one form to another. Some stories also acted as maps. In passing on the tale, one passed on information about different locations around the region. The story revealed how to get there and what one would find upon arrival. In that sense, some stories were like inventories of resources that could be harvested.

The storytelling tradition among the Mi'kmaq is still very much alive in the twenty-first century, but the stories are no longer those of "way back when." That's true of every culture on the planet. The narratives we come up with are a product of our experiences and tailored to the times in which we live.

We'd like to close this chapter with two stories whose roots go back into the mists of time. They are two different creation stories of the Mi'kmaq and how they came to be on Epekwitk. The first story is very much a product of more recent times, but the basis of the story is one that has been handed down across more generations than anyone can count. We respectfully acknowledge John Joe Sark, a Mi'kmaw Elder from Epekwitk and a *Keptin* of the Mi'kmaq Grand Council as the person who related something close to this version in a publication a few years back. We have edited it for inclusion here.

How Things Came to Be

Once, long ago, after the Great Spirit made all the things of earth, sea, and sky, the Creator turned to Kluskap (Glooscap) and said: "It's time to create people, I think."

The Great Spirit took a bow and shot an arrow into a tree, the sacred birch. The arrow struck the tree with a great noise, and its bark fell away.

The Great Spirit blew on the pieces of bark, turning them into children and women and men. They were the *L'nuk*, the people, and they were still asleep.

Next, the Great Spirit picked up a great handful of clay and said: "I will shape this earth into a crescent. It will be a home for the *L'nu*, Epekwitk. And the Great Spirit asked Kluskap to carry it to a special place beside the rest of the earth and out in the sea.

Kluskap carried Epekwitk and its sleeping people through the stars and the sky down to the blue water. With care he put the red clay down, like laying a cradle on the waves.

Kluskap took the bow the Great Spirit had given him, and he shot an arrow into the sacred tree. Again, the bark of the birch fell away. Its pieces became wigwams and canoes, bows and arrows, and everything else the *L'nu* would ever need.

The Great Spirit asked Kluskap to stay with the people and teach them not only to care for each other but also for what they had been given.

Kluskap flew above Epekwitk, up with Eagle, and from there he saw every tree and each animal, every bird and each bug. He came to know its waters and its fish, all medicines, too. He wept tears of joy at the creation and lay down on the warm sands of the shoreline and slept.

One summer, Kluskap woke, and he knew it was time to teach the people about the land they'd been given.

Kluskap taught them they were to share Epekwitk and its waters with one another and to see the work of the Great Spirit in all things in the seasons as they came.

Kluskap taught the people that they were equal with the animals. Epekwitk was for every creature, the large and the small.

And Kluskap showed the people their medicines. Where they were found, how to prepare them, and when they were used.

Kluskap taught the people to cherish their children and respect the Elders. For a long time Kluskap stayed with the people of Epekwitk, and it was good.

One autumn evening, Loon the messenger arrived and made warning sounds. Loon said a change was coming, and it was time for Kluskap to go. The Great Spirit was calling. So Kluskap flew away, but before he left he promised the people that one day he'd be back.

A quite different creation story for *Epewitk* came to our attention in Ruth Holmes Whitehead's wonderful book, *The Old Man Told Us*. According to Ruth's decades of research, this story is the oldest in the documentary record. It dates from 1933 and was recorded by Thomas Raddall, the famous Nova Scotian writer. Raddall collected it from two elderly Mi'kmaq, William Peminuit Paul and Mike Moko-ne (or McConney). How many generations back the story had been told and retold is impossible to know, but it certainly sounds and reads as though it was already centuries old by 1933. One of the many details to note is that in this tale there is no mention of Kluskap at all. The central figure is Sebanees. The following is the original version as it was recorded by Raddall.

I Will Sit in My Wigwam and Make Arrows for the Next Coming, by Michael William Francis (1923–1995). This painting is part of a series of murals depicting Mi'kmaw legends that Michael Francis, a Mi'kmaw artist originally from Big Cove, New Brunswick, was commissioned to create in 1972 on the walls of the Lennox Island parochial house. Photo courtesy John Joe Sark.

The Big Water Came and Drowned the Whole World

There was a man named Sebanees. It doesn't mean anything. It was just a name. Sebanees. It was in the el-time. [Note: "El-time" means "olden time."]

Sebanees was a quiet fellow. He was always thinking very deep. He lived by a lake, and he used to sit there and think and dream. One day there was a big Voice out of the Sky. Says, "Sebanees, there is going to be a big water. Big water will come up over everything, drown everything. This is because people do not believe your dreams."

Sebanees said, "Am I going to be drowned, too?"

The Voice said, "No, you will be saved, and all the people who believe what you say, and all the birds and fish and animals that you want."

Sebanees said, "How?"

And the Voice out of the Sky said: "Like this. There is going to be a big storm. Big flood. Now, you must watch the sky, Sebanees. You must gather all the people who believe in you, and all the birds and fish and animals, and you must watch the sky. You must gather here by the lake. When the sky right over your head turns colours like rainbow, only just red and kind of yellow, then you must do this. You must wade into the lake and take this whistle."

And he gave Sebanees a whistle made of wood. "Now, Sebanees, you must take this whistle and wade out into the lake and put the end of the whistle down into the water, and you must blow it. As you blow, there will freeze up out of the lake a boat made of ice. The more you blow the whistle, the boat will grow bigger. You must blow the ice boat big enough to hold all your people and birds and animals. You don't worry about the fish; they will be frozen up in the ice the same time as you blow up the boat. Then you must blow the whistle on all the birds and animals and they will go into the boat. Then you must put in all the people who believe in you because they will believe what you tell about the Big Water coming, and they will believe in your boat."

Sebanees did all these things. When the sky over his head turned red and kind of yellow, he began to blow his whistle, and the ice boat formed in the lake. And Sebanees went in the boat with the birds and animals and his people. And the Big Water came and drowned the world.

Well, they sailed around on the Big Water for a whole year. Then the water began to go away. The ground began to appear. The sun came back again and melted the ice boat, and all the fish and rocks and ground that had been frozen up in the ice boat stayed in that place. And that place was what you call Prince Edward's Island. And that is the story of Sebanees.

Now, here is the proof of this. Have you ever been to Prince Edward's Island? If you go, you will see that the rocks and the ground are different from the rocks and ground of any other place. That is because they were brought there in the ice boat of Sebanees. Now, the Micmac [Mi'kmaw] name today for Prince Edward's Island is Abegweit [Epekwitk]. That means like "the side of a boat when you see it a long way off and it seems to be low in the water."

But there is another, older, name for Prince Edward's Island among the Micmac people in the el-time .That is "Ookchiktoolnoo" [Kjiktu'lnu'], and it means, "our great boat."

The Mi'kmaq of the Island Today

Today there are about 1,100 Status* Mi'kmaq living on Prince Edward Island. That's up from a recorded low of 254 in the 1841 census. Half of the Island's Mi'kmaw population lives in one of four reserve communities: Lennox Island, Rocky Point, Scotchfort, or Morell. The others live off-reserve. Regardless of where they live, today's Mi'kmaq of Prince Edward Island belong to either the Lennox Island First Nation or the Abegweit First Nation. Those two bands have formed the Mi'kmaq Confederacy of Prince Edward Island to pursue projects of mutual interest, including this book and the travelling exhibit of the same name.

Though the Mi'kmaq are a relatively small percentage of Prince Edward Island's overall population, about 1 per cent, the place would not be the same without them. While their lives are as modern as other PEI peoples, at the same time they are the inheritors of a rich heritage that goes back a hundred centuries.

* The term "Status Indian" refers to those Aboriginal people—Mi'kmaq and many others—who are officially recognized by the federal government. In Prince Edward Island there are another thousand or so individuals who are of Mi'kmaw descent but who are not considered official "Status Indians."

Mi'kma'ki

The name "Mi'kma'ki" for traditional Mi'kmaw territory is relatively recent, though how far back the name goes is unknown. After all, the Mi'kmaq did not call themselves Mi'kmaq before the Europeans came; they accepted that name when it came along.

ALICE MITCHELL, BORN CIRCA 1877; DEATH DATE UNKNOWN

Alice Mitchell was born about 1877. Throughout her youth, she regularly camped on land at Rocky Point, as the Mi'kmaq had done for untold generations before her.

In 1892, John Newson, a non-Native farmer, purchased 470 acres of land from the Province of Prince Edward Island. His acquisition consisted of much of the Rocky Point peninsula. Despite the fact that there was widespread knowledge of regular use of the area by Mi'kmaw people over many generations, the deed of conveyance from PEI to John Newson made no mention of "Indian land" or "Indian rights" to the land. Such were the times.

Despite the land transaction, Mi'kmaw people continued to use the land. Records from 1912 show that the ownership and rights to the land in question were under dispute. Those Mi'kmaq who were associated with the Rocky Point land made representations to the Indian Affairs Branch. Their claim to the land must have been strong because John Newson is recorded as having been willing to pay the Mi'kmaq to relinquish their claim on the land. The dispute generated a good deal of correspondence between the Indian Affairs Branch and David Laird, the federal Minister of the Interior.

Enter Alice Mitchell. Through Charlottetown lawyers MacKinnon and McNeill, she made claim to the land in question and stated that the land had been used by her father, grandfather, and great-grandfather and that "Indians (were) never off that place."

In 1913, a three-acre lot was purchased by the federal government for the Mi'kmaq. However, the land was not the land that they had traditionally used in the area. Moreover, it was landlocked, so it was not suitable to their purposes and lifestyle, which had traditionally involved activities along the coast and shoreline. Alice and her brother Louis Mitchell responded that the land offered, three acres, was of poor quality. They refused to move from the land to which they were laying claim. The Department of Indian Affairs countered that they would construct houses if the "Indians" represented by Alice Mitchell would consent to move to the three-acre parcel purchased. During the period when reserves were being established and Aboriginal people were being centralized onto a select number of large reserves, Aboriginal people often accepted offers to move to unsuitable, poor-quality land in exchange for simple dwellings. In this case, however, Alice Mitchell stated that while the offer for houses was acceptable, the three-acre allocation was not. She stood her ground and refused to leave the land at Rocky Point.

In the face of Alice Mitchell's strong, principled stand, officials at the Department of Indian Affairs came to realize that the dispute would not be resolved by simply enticing Alice Mitchell with an alternative offer to forget her traditional claim to the land on Rocky Point. Largely as a result of Alice's efforts, in 1913, the Department of Indian Affairs purchased the land she claimed, three acres, for the creation of the Rocky Point Reserve as the last reserve on Prince Edward Island.

Once established, the reserve became home to more and more Mi'kmaw people. In 1914, Rocky Point was home to forty-eight Mi'kmaq. The growing population meant increasing numbers of children.

It was not long before the lack of a school became a major problem. Acting once again as a leader, Alice Mitchell began to speak out about this issue. She expressed to the local priest, a Fr. MacDonald, the need for structure and education for the youth. "They are running wild," she said, and further that she "cannot keep them under controle [sic] at all." In the absence of a schoolhouse, Alice even offered to let the children receive their instruction in her home. So it was that in October 1915, in the home of Alice Mitchell, that local teacher Peter Scully began the first formal education to take place at Rocky Point, with a class of nine students. This led to the construction of a modest schoolhouse, which opened in the fall of 1916.

Alice Mitchell was a woman of strong convictions and of courage. She was an early champion of Mi'kmaw rights on Prince Edward Island and a pioneer who helped shape the future of her community.

Rocky Point, circa 1900, group sitting outside wigwam. While we have no photos that show us the likeness of Alice Mitchell, this photo and several others like it were taken around 1900 by Charlottetown photographer A.W. Mitchell (no relation), on the Rocky Point land in question. It is possible that one of the young women in this photo is Alice Mitchell. Courtesy PARO.

We live in spiritual harmony
Wisdom gained from the minds of old
Revived in trails left for the young.
The path is still in existence
We practice it with respect

—Rita Joe, Mi'kmaw poet

Photo: John Sylvester

Cradle in the Sea
Epekwitk

The title of this second chapter is a poetic translation into English of a single Mi'kmaw word that linguists say might literally translate as "lying in the water." That the ancient name for Prince Edward Island can be rendered so poetically says a lot about the dynamic imagery inherent in the language of the Mi'kmaq. Mi'kmaq belongs to the Algonquian (also spelled as "Algonkian") family of languages. There are about thirty different languages in that broad grouping, belonging to peoples from the east coast of North America to the Rocky Mountains. The language of the Mi'kmaq is thought to have separated from that of the Maliseet about 2,600 years ago.

It is a treasure house where verbs are by far the most important article of speech. It's a tragedy that such a colourful and precise language—as well as a musical one—is no longer spoken by every Mi'kmaw. There are reasons for this loss, and they have to do with a long list of negative forces and influences inflicted upon the Mi'kmaq, especially in the nineteenth and twentieth centuries. In this chapter, however, we'd like to keep the focus on Epekwitk itself, or as the Mi'kmaw language has it, a piece of their territory that lies like a cradle in the sea.

We start by looking at the Island's place within the larger Mi'kmaw world. As mentioned earlier in the book, the Mi'kmaq have since time immemorial lived in all of what are today Nova Scotia and Prince Edward Island, in parts of New Brunswick, and on the Gaspé Peninsula of Quebec. Today there are also Mi'kmaq in eastern Maine and in Newfoundland, and some maintain that Newfoundland was also a part of the ancient territories as well. The customary interpretation has been that the vast swath of Mi'kmaw territory was divided or organized in seven districts.

In recent decades, the island of Newfoundland has sometimes been added to the mix as an eighth district, though some scholars maintain it should be seen as falling within the sphere of Unama'kik (or Cape Breton Island).

The English translations of the Mi'kmaw terms for those districts reveal how strikingly descriptive the Mi'kmaw names are.

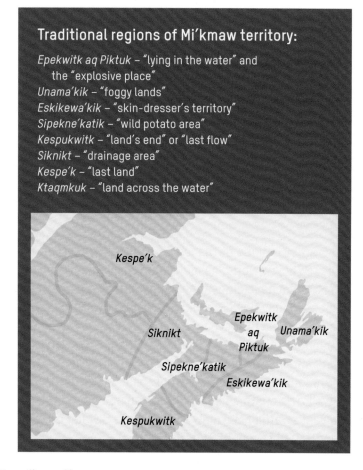

Traditional regions of Mi'kmaw territory:

Epekwitk aq Piktuk – "lying in the water" and the "explosive place"
Unama'kik – "foggy lands"
Eskikewa'kik – "skin-dresser's territory"
Sipekne'katik – "wild potato area"
Kespukwitk – "land's end" or "last flow"
Siknikt – "drainage area"
Kespe'k – "last land"
Ktaqmkuk – "land across the water"

Kespe'k

Siknikt

Epekwitk aq Piktuk

Unama'kik

Sipekne'katik

Eskikewa'kik

Kespukwitk

Land Surrounded by Water

Though Epekwitk became an island about five thousand years ago due to the combined effects of a rising sea level and crustal subsidence, ancient PEI was never a world apart. The Mi'kmaq who lived on the Island always saw themselves connected to the greater whole of Mi'kma'ki. Nothing reflected that wider vision better than the simple fact that the district in which they lived was composed of two parts. One part was Epekwitk, the cradle on the sea, while the other part, Pitukew'kik, was located on the other side of what today we call the Northumberland Strait. The full district was Epekwitk aq Pitukew'kik—Prince Edward Island and Pictou—and it had a common governance system.For the past few centuries the two parts of the district find themselves in two different Canadian provinces and separated by a body of flowing water, yet the waters of the strait were no big obstacle for the Mi'kmaq, who were accomplished travellers on water with their various canoes. They were known to travel great distances— even from Cape Breton Island to Newfoundland—in their large, seagoing canoes. Crossing the Northumberland Strait would have been a relatively easy paddle compared to that.

Early Europeans do not appear to have grasped the significance of the districts to the Mi'kmaq. Or, to put it differently, they did not think that the governance system in place among the Mi'kmaq (and other Aboriginal nations) had the same validity as their own approach to government. This was a common phenomenon across the Americas. The European newcomers could not see, or would not see, that the indigenous societies had their own long-standing ways of governing themselves and settling issues.

Those approaches simply differed from the more hierarchical, top-down approach common in Europe at that time. Some authors have gone so far as to claim that the much more "democratic" approaches to governance used by some Aboriginal societies were models and examples that over time the incoming European settlers would try to emulate. At the time of initial contact between the Mi'kmaq and representatives of various European states, a more egalitarian approach to governance was the last thing on most European minds.

The Europeans did not see the institutions with which they were familiar in the lands they encountered across the ocean. They saw no dominant kings and aristocracy, no formal church establishment like their own, and no law courts and punishment systems like they knew. A famous French shorthand description of that European point of view was "*ni roi, ni loi, ni foi*" ("no king, no law, no faith"). From this starting point the newcomers quickly concluded that the Mi'kmaq (and other Aboriginal peoples throughout the Americas) were living in a less developed state of social organization. Failing to recognize Mi'kmaw social structures, they proclaimed that the Aboriginal people they encountered had no valid government. From there it was a simple matter for Europeans to tell themselves Aboriginal people did not deserve their lands and that European people were justified in moving onto those traditional lands and imposing their European customs, values, and way of life. The Europeans' belief that God was on their side helped rationalize their colonizing thrust.

On Epekwitk, the arrival of European settlers came much later than in Nova Scotia (*Acadie*). In 1534, Jacques Cartier paid a fleeting visit to what he knew as Île Saint-Jean (PEI), coming ashore near the Island's western tip. That visit had no lasting consequences of any kind. As things worked out, the first year-round French and Acadian colonists did not come to the Island until 1720, nearly two hundred years later. So the Mi'kmaq of Epekwitk had many generations to get ready for the newcomers when they at last arrived. There can be little doubt that they heard stories about the Europeans and their ways from other Mi'kmaq in the region. At a minimum, chiefs and other Mi'kmaq would have held conversations when they met at their traditional summer gatherings and councils.

Before the arrival of populations of European descent, the single most important unit of governance in the traditional society of the Mi'kmaq was what history now calls the Grand Council (Sante' Mawio'mi). The Chiefs of all districts came together during the summer to discuss matters of common concern. The gatherings addressed issues relating to hunting and the harvesting of other resources, whether or not to go to war, and other issues of wide concern. All discussions were based on consensus and included mutual respect and trust as a code of governance. Such an approach to decision-making came to frustrate Europeans on many occasions. European societies at the time were mostly based on a top-down model, not on everyone being heard.

Grand Council (*Sante' Mawio'mi*)

The Mi'kmaq Grand Council is an ancient institution. However, its name in the Mi'kmaw language, *Sante' Mawio'mi,* reflects the close Mi'kmaw relationship with the French. The word *Sante'* comes from the French word for "holy" (*"sainte"*). This also suggests the importance of religion and faith in the work of the Grand Council, since the Mi'kmaq began adopting Christianity in 1610. Since the 1700s the representatives appointed to the Council are called *Keptinaq*. That term also derives from French, from the word *"capitaines."*

The *Sante' Mawio'mi* still exists in the twenty-first century but in altered form. There is still an overall *Kji-Saqmaw* (Grand Chief) and there are still *Keptinaq* (Captains) from all the districts. However, today the Grand Council's focus is on spiritual and cultural matters of all Mi'kma'ki. It leaves community development and politics to the chiefs and councils of individual First Nation communities. In 2013, Epekwitk is represented by two *Keptinaq* (Captains) on the Mi'kmaw Grand Council, John Joe Sark and James Bernard.

Flag of the Mi'kmaq Grand Council.

The mention of those summer get-togethers reminds us once again how much life in pre-contact times was based on the cycle of the seasons. It is only very recently in human history—and thanks to rapid long-distance travel, refrigeration, and greenhouses—that people can have access to a variety of fruits or vegetables all year long. It was not like that before about fifty years ago, nor any time earlier than that. In the many millennia of exclusive Mi'kmaw habitation on the Island, there was a definite rhythm and circular pattern to life. In the spring the Mi'kmaq came together in large groups along the lower rivers for salmon runs. In the summer they moved into smaller groups and lived along the bays and coasts. In the autumn they reassembled in large groups along the upper rivers for eel runs. When winter descended they moved inland in family groups and hunted and trapped the animals whose habits and habitats they knew well. The next spring, the cycle of life and sustainable movement was completed, ready to begin again.

"Our people feel a deep spiritual connection with Hog Island and the Sandhills. These islands in their natural state are part of our unbroken ties to this land, and to our ancestors. They are home to ancient sacred sites, which remain sacred to Mi'kmaq people today. We consider the Sandhills a Mi'kmaw Heritage Landscape." Board of Directors of the Mi'kmaq Confederacy of PEI, 2006.

The north shore of Epekwitk in winter.
Photo: John Sylvester

The extensive and ecologically rich dunes at the Hog Island Sandhills.
Photo: John Sylvester, copyright Mi'kmaq Confederacy of PEI.

Old sugar maples at Hog Island.
Photo: John Sylvester, copyright Mi'kmaq Confederacy of PEI.

Iron Rock at Hog Island and the Sandhills, a Mi'kmaw Heritage Landscape.
Photo: John Sylvester, copyright Mi'kmaq Confederacy of PEI.

An area on *Epekwitk* closely associated with the Mi'kmaq—and where their activities are well substantiated by the archaeological record—is Malpeque (*Malpek*) Bay. That great body of salt water is of high importance to all Mi'kmaq on the Island, not only those who live today at the Lennox Island First Nation located in the bay. The ancestors of all Island Mi'kmaq were living along its shores and harvesting food from its waters for many thousands of years. Hog Island, known in the Mi'kmaw language as *Pitawelkek*, is one of the extra special places on the bay. It holds evidence of ancient Mi'kmaw campsites, shell middens, burial grounds, and sacred sites. In 2006 the Board of Directors of the Mi'kmaq Confederacy of PEI declared it a Mi'kmaw Heritage Landscape. The Mi'kmaq Confederacy works on an ongoing basis with archaeologists and ecologists to preserve, protect, and understand Pitawelkek for all time.

Pre-contact ceramic from the Pitawelkek (Hog Island) site, excavated by Dr. Helen Kristmanson in 2012. The pot from which this piece came was decorated using a cord-wrapped stick to create repeating patterns around the rim. It dates from what is called the Late Woodland Period, about 1,350 years before present. Photo: Aboriginal Affairs Secretariat, Government of PEI.

Joe Abram, basket-maker, in the 1940s.
Photo courtesy Vincent Tuplin.

Today, Malpeque Bay is renowned on the Island for its beauty and its fishery. One of the best-known communities on the bay is Lennox Island. It is well-known both as a location and also as the name of one of PEI's two Mi'kmaw bands. The close identification of the Mi'kmaq with that particular location did not happen overnight. It's a story that begins as something of an oversight by British officialdom in the 1760s and then goes on with many twists and turns for a century and a half.

The story of the Mi'kmaq and Lennox Island begins, of course, thousands of years ago when the Mi'kmaq were already living on Malpeque Bay. However, its continuance as a Mi'kmaw community through colonial times, and to the present day, can be traced to the 1760s. It was then that British surveyor Samuel Holland was tasked by the imperial government to subdivide all of Prince Edward Island into large lots that were then to be auctioned off to absentee landlords in a lottery in England. In a remarkable undertaking of surveying at the time, Holland came up with sixty-seven lots. However, Holland did not include certain islands in his survey. One of the islands he overlooked was Lennox Island in Malpeque Bay.

Lennox Island Chief John T. Sark at a meeting of Atlantic Chiefs, circa 1900. Courtesy Public Archives and Records Office of PEI (PARO).

The Mi'kmaq on Malpeque Bay

The Canadian system of national historic designations covers three categories: persons, places, and events. In 1997, in the "event" category, the Historic Site and Monuments Board of Canada (HSMBC) recommended that the Mi'kmaq's ten thousand years of enduring use and settlement of Malpeque Bay be recognized for national significance. That presence and ongoing attachment to the bay is marked by an HSMBC plaque on Lennox Island.

Of course, the Mi'kmaq had no papers showing ownership of Lennox Island or any other part of PEI. That was not how their traditional society worked. In the new scheme of things, however, after the European systems were introduced, traditional use of an area counted for little in comparison with a deed. For seven decades, without success, the Mi'kmaw leadership on PEI and important non-Native sympathizers presented petitions to the colonial government of Prince Edward Island. They asked to have Lennox Island recognized as land for the Mi'kmaq to call their own. It wasn't much to ask, considering that all of Epekwitk had once been theirs.

Finally, the local Indian Agent, Theophilus Stewart, was able to involve a humanitarian group in Great Britain in the case. Stewart convinced the Aborigines Protection Society to purchase Lennox Island for what at the time was described as the "use of the Aboriginal Population of Prince Edward Island." It was not an action that placed the Mi'kmaq in control, but at least it was a step toward that ultimate goal. The British society put the island under a group of non-Native trustees. After nearly another half-century, in 1912 Lennox Island was placed under the federal government's Indian Act legislation. It was identified as a "Special Reserve."

Relaxing after Mass, Lennox Island, St. Anne's Sunday, 1930s. Photo courtesy Dave and Irene Haley.

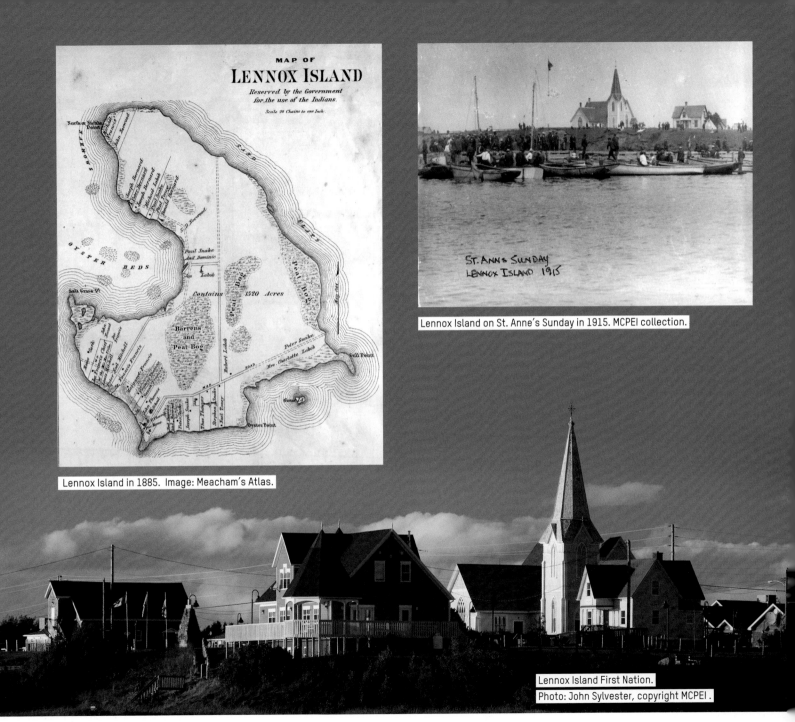

MAP OF
LENNOX ISLAND

Reserved by the Government
for the use of the Indians.

Scale 20 Chains to one Inch.

Contains 1520 Acres

OYSTER BEDS

Barrens and Peat Bog

Lennox Island in 1885. Image: Meacham's Atlas.

St. Ann's Sunday
Lennox Island 1915

Lennox Island on St. Anne's Sunday in 1915. MCPEI collection.

Lennox Island First Nation.
Photo: John Sylvester, copyright MCPEI.

Abegweit Becomes a Second Band

Though Prince Edward Island is the smallest Canadian province, it proved too large to have just the one band, identified with Lennox Island, to look after the interests of all the Mi'kmaq. In the early 1970s the Mi'kmaq who lived in the communities of Rocky Point, Scotchfort, and Morell Reserves found that they were not always able to attend meetings or events at Lennox Island. Their ability to travel with ease was made all the more complicated because there was no bridge from mainland PEI to Lennox Island until 1973. Regardless, as they put it at the time, they wanted to "have their own Council and conduct their own affairs."

A second Mi'kmaw First Nation came into existence in March 1972. Despite a raging snowstorm on the evening set for the final decision, all four Mi'kmaw communities on the Island came together at a public meeting to create the second band. Lennox Island First Nation was left intact, and the new second band's mandate was defined to represent the interests of the communities at Morell, Scotchfort, and Rocky Point. The federal government recognized that second grouping as the Abegweit First Nation.

Elder Bertha Francis and Chief Brian Francis cut the ribbon to open the Mawio'mi building on July 9, 2010, at the Abegweit Culture Centre in Scotchfort, PEI. Photo: Julie Pellisier-Lush.

Gathering of Abegweit Band and community members at Scotchfort for a fundraising walk called Great Strides. Photo: Julie Pellisier-Lush.

This gouge is a woodworking tool from what is known as the archaic period, from between 5,000 and 6,000 years ago. This was found in a farmer's field in Chelton, PEI, in the early twentieth century. The artifact was donated to the Mi'kmaq Confederacy of PEI by Lloyd Peterson and Chief Matilda Ramjattan. Photo: John Sylvester, copyright Mi'kmaq Confederacy of PEI.

Exposed shells and other faunal material at the Pitawelkek site, Hog Island. Photo: John Sylvester, copyright Mi'kmaq Confederacy of PEI.

Before we close this chapter we'd like to share a little bit about the many stories the Mi'kmaq have of long ago. Some are legends, others are recollections and memories recalled and handed down. The oral traditions are long and deep, and they shed light on the way things once were.

Elders hold an honoured place in Mi'kmaw culture; families and communities pay them great respect. Young Mi'kmaq listen carefully to what the Elders have to say. That's because they open windows into a world no longer here. Their stories teach lessons and values for life in the world today, but listeners have to find those lessons and values for themselves.

The ancient legends have been retold across many generations. There is great power in the old stories—and there are many lessons, too. The legends are often imbued with spirituality. In the oldest Mi'kmaw stories there are six worlds or levels of creation. In the story as it is being told, reality is fluid. People and animals can change and shift and move from one world to another and back again. Nor are spiritual and supernatural elements relegated to the past. There are many stories told in the Island's Mi'kmaw community of powerful and mysterious events that have taken place recently.

Ruth Holmes Whitehead, a leader in research on the Mi'kmaq, has studied many of their stories in her book, *Stories from the Six Worlds: Micmac Legends* (Halifax: Nimbus Publishing, 1988). Based on Whitehead's analysis, here are the six different worlds of the Mi'kmaq:

The World Above the Sky
(*Wskitqamu Kisoqe'k Musikiskituk*)

The World Above the Earth
(*Wskitqamu Kisoqe'k Wskitqamuminu*)

Earth World (*Wskitqamu*)

The Ghost World
(*Wskitqamu Skite'kmujueyey*)

The World Beneath the Water
(*Wskitqamu Samqwan*)

The World Beneath the Earth
(*Wskitqamu Pkewe'k Wskitqamuminu*)

Europeans found it difficult to grasp the complex spirituality and world view of the Mi'kmaq. Unfortunately, that meant they often tried to undermine it. We turn to that long, unhappy period in the history of the Mi'kmaq in the next chapter.

The Island We Call Home, *Mniku Ta'n Tel-Wi'tmek Nmitkinen*

Up and down this Island for as long as can be imagined, the Mi'kmaq raised their families and harvested the resources of land and sea. The entire island was their home. That being said, today's Mi'kmaq value some places more than others. These are special, even sacred, places. Sometimes a special location is where the living used to be particularly good; sometimes it is where ancestors lie buried.

Beach at Hog Island. Photo: John Sylvester, copyright Mi'kmaq Confederacy of PEI.

Hog Island (also known as George Island) and the Sandhills, a *Mi'kmaw Heritage Landscape*. Photo: John Sylvester, copyright Mi'kmaq Confederacy of PEI.

INDIAN SCHOOL.

The school at Lennox Island, under the charge of Martin Francis (Indian) as teacher, is doing well. There is no school in the County in which the pupils have to overcome the obstacle of a foreign accent, which is in such a satisfactory state. The pupils are exceedingly apt, industrious, and intelligent. The building now used as a school house is the residence of the teacher. The want of a proper school-room is much felt by the Indian community. These people feel very much interested in the Education of their children, and I think if the Government were to build them a suitable school house, that it would stimulate them to greater exertions.

TABULAR STATEMENT.

Number of schools examined,   75.

MARTIN FRANCIS, 1829–1878

We don't know a lot about Martin Francis, but what we do know paints a picture of a groundbreaking educator and highly capable Mi'kmaw man. He was the son of Magdalen Francis and John Francis. He was born around 1829, likely on or near Lennox Island.

We first see reference to him in the *School Visitor's Report* to the Colonial Government in the year 1842. That report states that residents of the Island, of all social classes, shared more or less equally in the benefits of education. The Island's Mi'kmaw population, however, continued to live a largely migratory lifestyle which meant that access to formal education was often intermittent.

Report on the excellent work of Martin Francis, from the Journal of the Prince Edward Island House of Assembly, 1870.

That report goes on to state, "A solitary exception...is an Indian Boy of 13 years of age, who has been receiving instructions during the last three years in different settlements around Richmond Bay, according as the migratory habits of the family led them in the vicinity of a school.... [T]he proficiency made by this boy—whose name is Martin Francis—proves that he is not inferior to other children in quickness of apprehension and capacity to learn."

Martin had a sound grasp of reading, writing, arithmetic, and fine penmanship. Furthermore, he was "devoting his leisure hours to the instruction of the other children of his Tribe." Francis was noted by the author as a bright young man who could be a positive influence and could serve as a role model for his Mi'kmaw peers.

Perhaps as a result of this glowing recommendation, the Acts of the colony's General Assembly show approval for "15 pounds to be provided for the education of Martin Francis, an Indian youth." It is not clear if Francis was able to take advantage of the scholarship funds approved. There is reason to believe that he may have returned to a more migratory life of hunting and fishing with his family.

Martin married Sally Thomas, daughter of Nancy Sark and John Thomas, on August 5, 1854, on Lennox Island.

When Lennox Island's first school began classes in 1868, Martin Francis was a resident of Lennox Island and became its first teacher. Since there was no school building, instruction took place in Martin's home.

In October of that year, an article appeared in the *Semi-Weekly Patriot*, an Island newspaper, wherein a visitor to the school relates the orderly workings of the classroom and the students' proficiency at reading.

In 1870, the report on schools recorded the excellent state of education on Lennox Island under the direction of Martin Francis. The report spoke of the solid achievement of the students in English, their second language, and suggested that the community would benefit greatly from having a schoolhouse.

By 1872, a formal request for a schoolhouse had been submitted to the government of Prince Edward Island. In 1875, a new schoolhouse was finally built. It is thought that the strong record of Martin Francis's teaching played a role in the decision to construct the new school.

Martin Francis taught at the Lennox Island School for ten years. On June 11, 1878, while teaching a class, he fell from his chair and was unable to move. He died two days later, of an apparent stroke. Martin Francis was a pioneer in Mi'kmaw education. He was the first Mi'kmaw schoolteacher in the entire Maritime Provinces.

This schoolhouse was built on Lennox Island in 1875 during Martin Francis's term as teacher there. Present in this photo, circa 1895–1900, are Chief John Sark, along with the teacher and pupils. Courtesy PARO.

I Lost My Talk

I lost my talk
The talk you took away
When I was a little girl
At Shubenacadie school
You snatched it away.
I speak like you
I think like you
I create like you
The scrambled ballad, about my word.
Two ways I talk
Both ways I say,
Your way is more powerful
So gently I offer my hand and ask,
Let me find my talk
So I can teach you about me.

—Rita Joe, Mi'kmaw poet

World Turned Upside Down

Boys from Lennox Island wait on the station platform for the train to take them to the Indian Residential School in Shubenacadie, Nova Scotia. The girls can be seen through the window, waiting inside the station. Circa 1935. Photo courtesy John Joe Sark / Vincent Tuplin.

Aboriginal comedians sometimes tell a joke: Did you hear the one about the guest who was once invited into the house—and ended up taking it over?

The joke succinctly encapsulates about four hundred years of history in Prince Edward Island, four centuries in which the guest—meaning newcomers who came mostly from Europe—slowly but surely came to control most of the land and resources across what had previously been the traditional territories of a good many Aboriginal people. As recently as the 1970s and 1980s, there was a broad consensus in mainstream society that the "displacement" of Aboriginal people was more or less inevitable and not really anybody's fault. The consensus was based on the implicit idea that Western civilization was stronger and superior and that Aboriginal people were bound to lose out. More recent analysis, however, has concluded that while specific advantages favoured the newcomers and greatly affected the way history played out, the advantages were not evidence of any kind of innate superiority on the part of the Europeans. In fact, most people now agree that there were many areas of life in which the Mi'kmaq and other Aboriginal peoples had superior systems and four hundred years ago were already doing things or expressing ideas that Europeans would only later come to embrace.

One huge factor in the European advance and the Aboriginal decline was that the newcomers brought with them germs and diseases previously unknown on this side of the Atlantic Ocean. The agriculture-based societies in which Europeans lived were favourable to the spread of communicable diseases—diseases to which they gradually built up some level of resistance. Those maladies and germs (colds, measles, and so on) still made Europeans sick, but when the diseases spread among Aboriginal peoples across the Americas their impact was devastating. Indigenous peoples of the Americas had no immunity whatsoever to many of the newly introduced germs. It is estimated that between 50 and 90 per cent of Aboriginal people died within a few decades after contact. Obviously, such a population loss greatly disrupted the traditional societies in every way imaginable. Among other effects, the diseases weakened the ability of the indigenous population to resist the incoming settlers once their numbers began to grow.

Another obvious factor was the difference in weaponry between the newcomers and the indigenous groups. European muskets and cannons had much more deadly effect than Aboriginal bows and arrows and spears. When some conflicts reached the battlefront, the playing field wasn't even close to being equal.

> Aboriginal: In the English language, the word goes back to the seventeenth century. Today's dictionaries define the term as meaning "first or earliest known, indigenous." Canada and Australia are the two countries that use the word most often. Section 35 of the Canadian Constitution states "the Aboriginal peoples of Canada include the Indian, Inuit and Métis peoples of Canada."

After the newcomers arrived and began to establish communities, it became clear that they had much different ideas about owning and using the land than the Mi'kmaq and other Aboriginal peoples had previously had. Living in harmony with nature—either as a philosophy or as a practical reality—was not a priority for most of the settlers of European descent. Settlers cleared forests and hunted certain animal species more intensely than ever before. We have more to say about the traditional Mi'kmaw view of their place in nature in Chapter 4.

As noted earlier in this book, the Europeans came from societies with a much more hierarchical social structure than the more egalitarian Mi'kmaq. They didn't value consultation and involvement in decision-making. In addition, the newly introduced Christian religion arrived around the same time as new ideas about governance and society. This religion held a definite attraction for at least some of the Mi'kmaq.

The first to embrace Roman Catholicism was the great leader Membertou and his family in 1610. Membertou likely took this step at that time for strategic and practical reasons—possibly even for simple hospitality. To be sure, Membertou and other early converts to Christianity did not leave their traditional spiritual beliefs and practices behind. Rather, they practised a kind of syncretism, or blending of different faiths, in their spiritual lives. Other Mi'kmaq similarly added Christianity to their belief system in the years that followed, again blending elements from the different ways of understanding the world. In some cases, the shift to Christianity took decades or even a century.

Part of the attraction of the new religion was likely that it seemed to arrive alongside the metal objects and incredibly useful muskets of the newcomers. Also, many Mi'kmaq may have believed that Christianity helped protect its adherents from the diseases that were decimating Aboriginal populations. By converting, they hoped to gain a share of protection and resilience.

The result of all these changes—the widespread illness and mortality, the new weapons and tools, the new peoples coming in larger numbers all the time—was, over time, to turn the traditional world of the Mi'kmaq (and other peoples across the continent) upside down. That the Mi'kmaq dealt with those changes, and kept their values and traditions alive as they did, is a story not of defeat but of remarkable adaptation and accomplishment.

It used to be that the Mi'kmaq were rarely even mentioned in history books, except as obstacles to the settlement of the land by either French or English colonists or both. Today, however, historians no longer consign the Mi'kmaq to the margins of the colonial period. Professor John Reid of St. Mary's University, among others, has pointed out that throughout the 1600s and well into the 1700s, what we call the Maritimes was in reality more under Mi'kmaw control than British, French, or Acadian control. However, it was eventually the populations of European descent who obtained the upper hand. They came to dominate the population in their numbers and their institutions.

Drawing attributed to Father LeClerq or Father Jumeau, Gaspésie, late seventeenth century, from a 1692 edition of LeClerq's Nouvelle Relation de la Gaspesie. Image courtesy the Champlain Society, Toronto, Ontario.

The arrival of thousands of New England Planters began an influx into the region, and that tide of immigration grew much larger still with the coming of Scots, Irish, and English settlers and United Empire Loyalists from the American colonies. A significant number of Loyalists coming to the Maritimes were free Blacks. There were also many slaves of African descent. The nature of Mi'kmaw relationships with settlers was affected by wars and territorial rivalries between European empires. The most intense period of European imperial rivalry was a 150-year period spanning much of the seventeenth and eighteenth centuries. Generally speaking, the Mi'kmaq chose to ally themselves with the French against the British in colonial wars. There were at least two and sometimes three reasons for that stance. The first reason was that the Mi'kmaq found that the French showed more respect for their chiefs and social values than did the British. By the eighteenth century, most if not all Mi'kmaw chiefs were participating in annual gift-giving ceremonies with the French. Those were meetings that officially renewed ties between the two peoples. A second reason was that beginning in the 1600s and continuing in the 1700s, most Mi'kmaq became Roman Catholics. That was also the religion of the French and Acadians. Many British were Protestants and hostile to the Catholic faith. While many Roman Catholic Scottish and Irish settlers came to Prince Edward Island beginning in the 1770s, those communities generally did not form the same deep relationship with the Mi'kmaq as had the French and Acadians beginning in 1720. A third reason is that sometimes there was inter-marriage between Mi'kmaw and the French and Acadians. That meant there were in some families blood ties between the two peoples.

On Epekwitk, gift-giving ceremonies between Mi'kmaq and French took place annually for several decades at Port-la-Joye (the old French name for what is today called Charlottetown Harbour). Beginning in 1720, there was a small French fort and community of Port-la-Joye right beside what is now the Rocky Point reserve. The location of the meetings is now a national historic site administered by Parks Canada. Its official name is Port-La-Joye–Fort Amherst. Fort Amherst is the name the location was given in 1758, when the British arrived on the Island to remove the French administration and deport 3,500 Acadians to France.

Mi'kmaw woman and Abbé Maillard. Image: Francis Back, courtesy Parks Canada.

The Mi'kmaw name for the Port-la-Joye location is Skmaqan, which means "waiting place." That name is thought to come from the fact that sometimes the Mi'kmaq had to wait for several days for French leaders to arrive from Louisbourg for the ceremonies that confirmed their shared alliance. In 1734, the wait was almost a month.

In the period before 1758, the Mi'kmaq often found it necessary to take up arms to defend their traditional territories. At this time, the enemy was inevitably the British. This was not because their allies the French told the Mi'kmaq what to do or how to fight. On the contrary, the Mi'kmaq had absolute control over who and when and if they were to fight. However, the alliance celebrated in annual ceremonies between 1720 and 1758 at Port-la-Joye most definitely had a military dimension. The French hoped the Mi'kmaq would conduct raids, capture vessels, and carry on armed conflicts against the British on and around Île Saint-Jean. And indeed, Mi'kmaq participated in conflicts, such as one at Port-la-Joye in July 1746 that involved significant loss of life. On land, the Mi'kmaq sometimes viewed British soldiers and settlements as threats and engaged them in battle. But the Mi'kmaq were also extremely adept at sea, something about which the history books have not said very much.

Mi'kmaw warriors captured dozens—that's right, dozens—of New England schooners and other sailing vessels. They would turn the vessels against other New England ships in turn or else scuttle them.

Mi'kmaw warrior, circa 1730, as described in French journals. Image: Francis Back, courtesy Parks Canada.

For many people, the most shocking part of the wars in the eighteenth century concerns some of the horrendous methods employed as part of warfare. Brutality was used on all sides. The British greatly feared what Mi'kmaw warriors could do to their soldiers and civilians, especially in attacks that caught them unawares. In their fear of the Mi'kmaq, and after a raid on the new settlement of Dartmouth, the British administration in Nova Scotia paid bounties for Mi'kmaw scalps, of men, women, and children. That this terrible measure became law is deplorable. However, the French allies at Louisbourg similarly paid bounties for scalps, only in this case, the bounty was on British scalps, and the French paid their rewards to Mi'kmaw warriors. It was a truly terrible time.

Despite the fear, mistrust, and generally dreadful relations that existed between the Mi'kmaq and the British for many decades, out of that long conflict there came one good: treaties that the Mi'kmaq signed with representatives of the British Crown. Treaties were something the Mi'kmaq had never pursued or signed with the French; they were allies. The British, however, were longtime enemies, so formal treaties seemed like a good idea. History has proven the wisdom of treaties: they were very much a good idea. Admittedly, the historical treaties signed in the eighteenth century were long ignored or forgotten by later governments, but the Mi'kmaq never forgot. And treaties never lost their status as law. Since then, both individual treaties and the overall treaty process behind have been validated by the Supreme Court of Canada. As a result, the treaties are not dead; they are still very much in force.

The treaty process took place over quite a few years. The list below highlights specific dates and a few details. The single most important detail of all these treaties remains that at no time did the Mi'kmaq cede any of their traditional lands. They did not cede any of PEI or Nova Scotia, nor a good part of New Brunswick, nor a portion of Quebec. The agreements were only about "peace and friendship" between the two peoples: never land. The treaties allowed for full access to hunting grounds so the Mi'kmaq could continue their traditional ways without interference.

1725: The Mi'kmaq and other First Nations sign a treaty at Boston, Massachusetts.

1726–28: The Mi'kmaq ratify the 1725 treaty at Annapolis Royal, NS.

1752: The Mi'kmaq sign a treaty in Halifax, NS.

1760–61: The Mi'kmaq sign a treaty in Halifax, NS.

1776: The Mi'kmaq sign a "Treaty of Alliance and Friendship" with the State of Massachusetts Bay, at Watertown, Massachusetts.

Treaties have often been in the news in the past few decades. That's because they are not dead, historical documents in some archive, but living agreements that are still valid. A series of decisions by the Supreme Court of Canada has upheld the validity of the treaties the Mi'kmaq signed with representatives of the Crown. In turn, that series of decisions has affirmed and helped to define the Aboriginal and treaty rights of the Mi'kmaq as recognized in the Canadian constitution.

The Canadian Constitution Act of 1982 states: "The existing aboriginal and treaty rights of the aboriginal peoples of Canada are hereby recognized and affirmed."

There have been several landmark decisions by the Supreme Court of Canada that have had particular impact on Aboriginal and treaty rights. Several of these decisions have had significant effect on the lives of the Mi'kmaq of Prince Edward Island.

In 1990, in what is known as the *Sparrow decision*, the Supreme Court upheld Aboriginal and treaty rights by agreeing that Aboriginal people in Canada had the right to fish for food, social, and ceremonial purposes. The Supreme Court went on to say that First Nations "have a priority over other uses of the fishery, including commercial fishing, but these rights are subject to overriding considerations such as conservation."

In 1999, the Supreme Court's *Marshall decision* went further to indicate that the First Nations had the "treaty right to hunt, fish, and gather in pursuit of a moderate livelihood based on local treaties signed in the eighteenth century. In other words, communities fishing under these treaties may sell their catch." However, the federal government reserved the right to regulate the fishery with a view to conservation. The increased access to the commercial fishery that resulted from the *Marshall decision* has been a major economic boost to PEI Mi'kmaw communities.

In the past, even until about ten years ago, federal and provincial governments would often undertake actions and projects with little regard as to their potential effect upon Aboriginal and treaty rights. However, in decisions such as *Haida Taku,* in 2004, the Supreme Court has stated that where there is a possibility that these rights may be infringed upon, federal and provincial governments have a duty to consult and, where appropriate, accommodate the affected First Nations.

Lennox Island, circa 1960. Left to right: Leo Daley, Indian Agent; unidentified man employed with Indian Affairs Branch; Louie Mitchell, Councillor; Joe Tuplin, Councillor; and Frank Jadis, Chief. Courtesy Graham Tuplin.

This has become commonly referred to as the "duty to consult" and has meant much more frequent and meaningful involvement and input of First Nations into government decisions and actions. The Court directions on the duty to consult and on "accommodation, where appropriate" have effectively meant that Aboriginal and treaty rights must be taken into account; they no longer simply are considered when convenient.

In recent years, Mi'kmaq governments have been entering into progressive agreements with federal and provincial governments. For example, in 2007 the First Nations signed a Partnership Agreement with the federal and provincial governments as a way to mutually identify areas of strategic priority in improving life outcomes for PEI Mi'kmaq. More recently, on August 13, 2012, Island Chiefs signed an agreement with PEI Premier Robert Ghiz and federal Minister for Aboriginal Affairs and Northern Development Canada John Duncan regarding an agreed process for consultation among the parties.

A tarpaper shack, Northam, PEI, 1945-1947.
Photo courtesy Vincent Tuplin.

Poverty

For many Mi'kmaq, the nineteenth and early twentieth century was a time of grinding poverty. Traditional hunting no longer could provide as it had previously, and the wealth of the non-Aboriginal society was largely inaccessible. The tragic situation is expressed here in a letter that appeared in the *Summerside Progress* of January 4, 1869:

> "Fifty years ago the Micmac was better off in this Island than he is today. Then he had large forests through which to roam in search of game and wild animals, as well as the choice wood and other material requisite for his work, and abundance of firewood, all of which he could seek and use without molestation or denial...but now, poor Micmac!— the times are very different...."

Prior to the treaty-based and rights-based protocols and arrangements of the past few decades, similar respectful negotiations were not present for many, many years. In these years without respect, throughout the nineteenth century and well into the twentieth century, the Mi'kmaq had to put up with prejudices and hostility that have only recently become unacceptable in our much-changed world. Although in every time period the Mi'kmaq had friends in mainstream society, for many generations those allies and supporters were few and far between.

For a couple of centuries or more, many in the mainstream society thought the Mi'kmaq were a quaint curiosity. Many predicted that they would disappear. Even some would-be supporters believed that cultural assimilation was the best course, a belief with devastating effects.

Worse than the day-to-day prejudice they experienced, prejudice embedded in public policy caused Mi'kmaq to lose control over where and how they lived. They became wards of the state, defined by a government whose stated intent was to "take the Indian-ness out of the Indian." Laws created in the mid-1800s applied new sets of rules. Some legislation defined who were Indian people and who weren't and what they could and couldn't do. Other legislation discouraged and forbade traditional medicines, customs, and languages. Such restrictions lasted for over a century. More bad news was to come: from the 1930s to the 1960s many Mi'kmaw children were transported off the Island, away from their families, to a residential school in Shubenacadie, Nova Scotia. This was a tragedy with long-lasting impacts on the Mi'kmaw language and culture. An entire generation was cut off from their roots and their traditions.

Another harmful policy of governments toward the Mi'kmaq was "centralization." In the 1940s and 1950s, governments adopted a policy to move all Mi'kmaw families from where they were living to fewer locations, where they could more easily be counted and controlled. The policy cut off relocated people from many places their ancestors had long known and from ancient ways of living on the land.

Canada's Apology to All Aboriginal People for Residential Schools

"The treatment of children [in Indian residential schools] is a sad chapter in our history. For over a century, Indian residential schools separated over 150,000 aboriginal children from their families and communities... Today, we recognize that this policy of assimilation was wrong, has caused great harm, and has no place in our country...To the approximately 80,000 living former students, and all family members and communities, the government of Canada now recognizes that it was wrong to forcibly remove children from their homes and we apologize for having done this."

—Prime Minister Stephen Harper, June 11, 2008

For Mi'kmaq, the heartaches and hardships of the past are many—too many to count. But Mi'kmaq are still here, vigorous and proud on Epekwitk, and standing on their feet.

Children in front of a camp at Rocky Point, about 1898. Charlottetown can be seen on the horizon. This photo was taken by A.W. Mitchell, a fine amateur photographer, who photographed many Mi'kmaw individuals and families on PEI between 1895 and 1910. Photo: A.W. Mitchell, courtesy PARO.

Indian Residential School at Shubenacadie, Nova Scotia.
Photo courtesy Sisters of Charity, Halifax Congregational Archives.

A Shaman Speaks, Port-la-Joye, Circa 1740

Pierre Maillard was a Roman Catholic priest, born in France around 1710 and educated in Paris. In 1735, he came to lead religious missions and work among the Mi'kmaq, mostly in Île Royale (now called Cape Breton) but also in Île Saint-Jean (now Prince Edward Island).

In a long letter that Maillard wrote around 1755, he describes a meeting and discussion with a famous Mi'kmaw shaman called L'kimu (pronounced Ulgimoo and spelled "Arguimaut" by Maillard, and also seen as "Alguimou," "Arguimeau," and so on). He dates the conversation to about the year 1740 and describes their location as seated in a wigwam at Port-la-Joye. L'kimu was a powerful and respected shaman, influential among the Mi'kmaq and alternately feared and respected by the French. Among stories that added to the mystique of L'kimu were those that stated he had died and come back from the dead. Maillard asks L'kimu: "How did you live in this region before the arrival of Europeans?" L'kimu replies:

> Father, before your arrival in these parts where God decreed we should be born and where we have grown like the grasses and the trees you see around you, our most constant occupation was to hunt all sorts of animals so as to eat of their flesh and to cover ourselves with their skins. We hunted both small and large game-birds and chose the best and the most beautifully feathered birds to make ornaments for our heads. We killed only enough animals and birds to sustain us for one day, and then, the next day, we set out again.

> But never think that our hunting was as arduous as it is today. All we needed to do in those times was to leave our wigwams, sometimes with our arrows and spears and sometimes without, and at a very short distance from our village we would find all we needed.

L'kimu goes on to tell Maillard how fires were lit and the rituals around keeping a fire lit through the winter—a very important job.

> To preserve the fire, especially in winter, we would entrust it to the care of our war-chief's women, who took turns to preserve the spark, using half-rotten pine wood covered with ash. Sometimes this fire lasted up to three moons. When it lasted the span of three moons, the fire became sacred and magical to us, and we showered with a thousand praises the chief's woman who had been the fire's guardian during the last days of the third moon. We would all gather together and, so that no member of the families which had camped there since the autumn should be absent, we sent out young men to fetch those who were missing. Then, when our numbers were complete, we would gather round and, without regard to rank or age, light our pipes at the fire. We would suck in the smoke and keep it in our mouths, and one by one we would puff it out into the face of the woman who had last preserved the spark, telling her that she was worthy above all to share in the benign influence of the Father of Light, the Sun, because she had so skillfully preserved His emanations.

L'kimu relates how food was cooked and describes sacred customs regarding the leftover bones of animals whose flesh had been eaten. He tells of the building of canoes, both from birch bark and hides. L'kimu describes terrible flesh-eating fish that would attack the canoes:

> We have had our canoes, Father, from time immemorial, and they have always been the same as you see now. In olden times, instead of the birchbark we use now, our ancestors used moose skins, from which they had plucked the hair and which they had scraped and rubbed so thoroughly that they were like your finest skins. They soaked them several times in oil and then they placed them on the canoe frame, just as we do with birchbark today, fitted them, stretched them, and fixed them by sewing them, sometimes with animal tendons, sometimes with spruce roots, and thus they sailed from the coast to a nearby island without ever going too far away from the shore...never further than seven or eight leagues....
>
> These are long journeys for us. We much prefer to make them in calm or good weather, since the Bad Fish that often infest these seas do not allow us to sail without worry and fear. All too often, these malicious beings [believed to be either killer whales or sharks] attack the sterns of our canoes so suddenly and without warning that they sink the boat and all who are in it. Some escape by swimming, but there are always some who fall prey to these voracious flesh-eating fish. When we see them bearing down on us, we stop paddling immediately, and, taking a pole tipped with a very hard pointed bone, we try to harpoon the fish if we can.

> As soon as it feels the wound, the creature draws off for a time. We take advantage of the short respite to paddle as fast as we can; and if it returns to the attack we repeat our actions until we see land. There is almost no way to escape if two animals attack the canoe at the same time. If we are caught without our spears, with fear and trembling we throw overboard any pieces of meat or fish we may have, one by one, to distract the fish behind us while the one in front paddles gently on without stopping. If we have nothing else to throw we take off our furs and throw them overboard. We have often thrown even our game-bird headdresses to the creatures. At last, when there is nothing left to throw, we take the longest and sharpest of the bones we always have in our canoes and tie them as best we can to the ends of our paddles. Or else we tie several arrows together, binding the points as tightly as we can, and tie the bundle to the end of a paddle or an oar with a belt. Then we lie in wait to harpoon the creature. Of course, it is not as easy to harpoon the animal with this weapon as with the spear, because the paddle is never long enough. However, this makeshift weapon has often served us well. Finally, when we have to make a journey (which we do rarely because of these fearsome animals), we take several very leafy branches and put them at the stern of our canoe, where they stick up about two feet above the rim. We know by experience that when these fish see and catch the scent of the branches, they draw away and do not come near us. Apparently they think it is a piece of land where they could become stranded.

L'kimu and several other "old men" with him had recently been baptized into the Roman Catholic faith (though they had yet to make their first communion). L'Kimu goes on to ask Father Maillard about the origin of the Christian prayers that he and the other men are learning.

This conversation gives us a glimpse into a world and a way of life that already by 1740 had changed much and was continuing to change rapidly. The letter is of great historical value, being the only existing record where a named Mi'kmaw of the era describes, in his own words, what life was like before the arrival of Europeans.

Puinoq, The Shaman, by Roger Simon. Image courtesy Vienna Sanipass and Metepenagiag Heritage Park.

Making Containers: Both an Art and a Practical Skill

Containers were essential to a people who moved often and needed to transport belongings and food supplies. The work of making containers was typically done by women. Basket-making was and continues to be a very important aspect of Mi'kmaw culture. In pre-contact times Mi'kmaq fashioned many types of containers—including bags, baskets, and bowls from a wide variety of locally available materials such as reeds, grasses, bark, and possibly wood-splints. Earthenware ceramic pottery appears to have made its first appearance in the Maritimes about 2,500 to 3,500 years ago. The earliest known piece of ceramics found in PEI dates from about 2,150 years ago. It was found on Hog Island. After their introduction, ceramics became an important tradition.

Perhaps the most versatile and widely used material for containers was birchbark. Strong, pliable, hard-wearing, and resistant to rot and insects, it could be sewn using spruce root and fashioned into many things. Birchbark is naturally waterproof and can hold water if the seams are caulked.

The Mi'kmaw tradition of creating ornate decorative patterns using paint, embroidery, etching, or other techniques helped beautify clothing and many objects used in daily life. Containers are often excellent examples of these decorative arts.

Mi'kmaw women were also skilled weavers. They used various materials to create rich patterns and textures. In the nineteenth and twentieth centuries, these weaving and basket-making traditions assumed a new role in the life of many Mi'kmaq. As settler populations grew and more and more land was cleared for agriculture, there was a steady demand for the strong, wood-splint baskets made quickly and cheaply by the Mi'kmaq. The baskets were highly sought after for their usefulness in harvesting crops, particularly potatoes and apples. This new market for baskets suited the Mi'kmaw lifestyle of the time. The baskets could be made almost anywhere, and the maple and ash trees needed to make the baskets were widely available. Basket-makers would camp near an ash grove near a town, then, when they had sold enough baskets, would move on to another grove near another town. The market demand for baskets was widespread, with farmers needing potato baskets in every part of Prince Edward Island. Basket-making became a portable way to supplement one's living and earn money by producing a needed product. It is probably the ubiquity of the potato baskets that introduced many people to Mi'kmaq basketry and opened up a market for more elaborate "fancy" baskets.

Perhaps the greatest expression of traditional Mi'kmaw artistry and embellishment is to be found in the use of porcupine quills. Quillwork has been called the signature art of the Mi'kmaq. Traditionally, quills were dyed using plants. Shades of brown, green, red, black, and gold were common. The use of the brilliant white undyed quills also is seen. While porcupines are not indigenous to Prince Edward Island and have never been found here, there is a tradition of quillwork on the Island. The examples pictured here come from the collection of the Prince Edward Island Museum and Heritage Foundation.

Mi'kmaw quillwork, nineteenth century, from the collection of the Prince Edward Island Museum and Heritage Foundation. Photo: John Sylvester, copyright Mi'kmaq Confederacy of PEI.

Mi'kmaw quillwork, nineteenth century, from the collection of the Prince Edward Island Museum and Heritage Foundation. Photos: John Sylvester, copyright Mi'kmaq Confederacy of PEI.

Baskets by David and Dorothy Bernard, from the Ray Sark Collection of Mi'kmaw baskets. Photo: John Sylvester, courtesy Fran Sark, John Sylvester, and Ron Walsh.

PEI Mi'kmaw fancy basket with jik aji'j ("snail") curls from the collection of the Prince Edward Island Museum and Heritage Foundation. Photo: John Sylvester, copyright MCPEI.

Charlie Sark binds the edge of a basket, from the Ray Sark Collection of Mi'kmaw baskets. Photo: John Sylvester, courtesy Fran Sark, John Sylvester, and Ron Walsh.

Basket-maker David Bernard. Photo courtesy Fran Sark.

JOE TUPLIN, 1889–1983

In 1889, a young unmarried woman (of European descent) from the vicinity of Grand River, PEI, became pregnant. As was common at the time, her family was sensitive to the embarrassment that could fall upon an unwed mother and her family. Soon after the baby boy's birth, the baby in question was quietly given to two elderly women who had agreed to raise and care for him in their home on Lennox Island. The boy's name was Joe Tuplin.

Joe Tuplin as a young man.
Courtesy Grace Nelson collection.

Raised in the close-knit and then somewhat isolated community, Joe first learned the Mi'kmaw language. He grew to become an active and respected community member on Lennox Island and in 1911 he married Mary Anne Snake (Peters), also from Lennox Island, and they had seven children.

Joe enlisted to serve in World War I. He served almost the full duration of the war before being wounded and returning to Lennox Island to work his small mixed farm with his family. His wife Mary Anne suffered poor health and was often confined to bed. She died in 1933 at thirty-eight years of age. Subsequently, most of their children were sent to residential school in Shubenacadie, Nova Scotia.

Joe's children, Basil and Mary, 1920.
Courtesy Grace Nelson collection.

In 1934 Joe remarried, and Sarah Mitchell of Lennox Island became his wife. Together they had five children. Joe continued to be a successful and hard-working farmer until 1939 when he joined the World War II effort, serving this time as a guard at a prisoner-of-war camp. After the war, Joe again returned to Lennox Island to farm and fish.

In 1951, after growing up on Lennox Island and spending sixty-one years living there, Joe Tuplin was forced to leave his home when a regulation in the Indian Act, which meant that Joe was considered non-Aboriginal, was enforced. He moved first to Rocky Point and then to Lower Montague, PEI, where he lived the rest of his years with his wife Sarah. Joe Tuplin died in 1983. He was ninety-three years old.

Joe is remembered as a kind, generous, and hard-working man and a devoted father. On many occasions he was known to quietly provide produce from his farm to those going through hard times. He is remembered by Mi'kmaw speakers as a man who spoke eloquently and possessed many fine old words in his Mi'kmaw vocabulary.

Joe Tuplin was a man proud of his Mi'kmaw upbringing, his family, and his community.

Joe and his family.
Courtesy Grace Nelson collection.

Wartime telegram informing family that Joe Tuplin had been wounded. Courtesy Grace Nelson collection.

"Come right away." Telegram from Joe Tuplin to his wife announcing his return from World War I. Courtesy Grace Nelson collection.

Old Stories

There are stories told by the elderly
Of bannock baked in a bed of stone
Of birchbark fashioned into a pot
To boil meat and bone

There are tales told
Of what life was like before
Of wigwam in the wood
With deerskin for a door

Fishing from canoe
Hunting in the wild
Herbs gathered for the sick
To cure and soothe

Prayers and song
Memories told to the young
When all life was Lnua'kis

It will never be the same again
Only in our minds and elderly tales

—Rita Joe, Mi'kmaw poet

Part of Nature's Fabric

Kesikn Ta'n Teltaqte'kasik Wskitqamu

It is easy to romanticize times gone by. Nearly everyone has done so with recollections of their own past. We may select certain memories and forget (or suppress) anything that does not fit the picture that we prefer. So, too, societies sometimes imbue an era with a golden glow it almost certainly did not have as the society's members (or their predecessors) lived through it at the time. Nostalgia is likely where the expression "good old days" comes from.

Mi'kmaw Encampment at Point Levis, Quebec by James Pattison Cockburn (1779–1847), painted about 1840. Copyright McCord Museum.

Our challenge in this chapter is to share some of what we have learned about an aspect of traditional Mi'kmaw life that can easily be romanticized: the people's connection to nature. Life in the millennia before there was electricity, refrigeration, motorized transportation, or multi-functional tools could be extremely hard. But looking backwards from the fast-paced, resource-depleting lifestyle most of us follow in today's western world, there is something very appealing about an era and a way of life that did not include some of the negative consequences we witness. As we discuss that earlier era in the paragraphs that follow, we leave it to the reader to find the balance between reality and myth. One point is beyond debate: in traditional times, which lasted millennia, the Mi'kmaq of Epekwitk and in other parts of Mi'kma'ki saw themselves much more as a part of nature's fabric than most of us do today.

The early Europeans considered the Mi'kmaq they encountered in Atlantic Canada much different from themselves in many ways. One quality that especially intrigued the early explorers and settlers, and that they observed and commented on, was the Mi'kmaw law of respect for the Great Spirit and for the animals, including fish and birds. It was a respect the Europeans often did not share. They, for the most part, saw animals as something to eat and maybe make a profit on.

Though few Europeans were inclined to see it, there were reasons behind the profound Mi'kmaw philosophy of respect for wildlife. The Mi'kmaq of that traditional era felt an extremely close connection to that from which they gained their sustenance. There were no stores or warehouses nor any supply ships coming to bring them provisions. Their food and their medicines, their clothing and their weapons and tools: everything came from where they lived. They either harvested it as it was or transformed it through their labours and their skills to make it useful to themselves. There was little or no separation between the people and the natural world in which they lived. Humankind was not above the rest of creation, but a part of it. In the European world view of the time, the human species had been given dominion over all. By contrast, the ancient Mi'kmaq believed every species, including the human species, lived in cycles, and every creature deserved respect for what it contributed.

The traditional Mi'kmaw perspective was that just as there was a Mother Earth, so too, was there a Father Sun. In this view of life and the world, balance was important. That balance was to be found in all aspects of life: between the genders, among all the species, and with all ecosystems. Everyone, animals and fish and insects included, had a place in the circle of life.

The people tried to take no more than they needed, and they respected what they used. This is a philosophy that a growing number of people in the twenty-first century are returning to, but in colonial times it was not well regarded at all. The early fishermen and fur traders of European descent did not share the Mi'kmaw view. Their top priority was the short-term value of the resources they encountered, whether those "resources" were plants, humans, or other animals.

Understandably, the coming of the newcomers introduced a few cracks in some of the ancient ways and views of the Mi'kmaq. The fur trade, for instance, encouraged over-hunting. To obtain European iron pots and tools and fabric, and decorative items as well, the Mi'kmaq and other Aboriginal peoples in North America began to harvest many more beavers and other animals than they had ever taken before. Balance among the different ecosystems began to slip away, along with restraint.

With the coming of permanent European settlements, trees began to fall in ways not seen before. The newcomers needed wood to build their dwellings, forts, and vessels, and firewood to burn to cook and keep themselves warm. The ancient circle of sustainability was challenged and began to come undone.

These changes in the environment had deep effects upon the Mi'kmaq during the nineteenth century. It was a time when PEI Mi'kmaq were becoming more integrated into European lifestyles. Some Mi'kmaq began to adopt farming as a lifestyle. However, it was also a time when hunting and fishing, upon which most depended, became much more difficult due to displacement of wildlife and habitat loss. Near starvation was common.

One of the best illustrations of the cyclical nature of traditional Mi'kmaw life is found in the names they gave to the months of the year. Though today's European-derived calendar is divided into twelve months, there are thirteen full moons in every year. The Mi'kmaq had a different name for each period of 28 days, and each name related to what was happening in the natural world. The old Mi'kmaw name for the thirteenth month seems to have faded from their collective memory, so long have they been using the twelve-month calendar of the Europeans. The year began and ended in the spring, around what we now call March.

What follows is the thirteen-month Mi'kmaw lunar calendar, which runs from March to March.

Mi'kmaw Name	English Translation
Si'ko'ku's	Maple Sugar Moon (March–spring)
Pnatmuiku's	Egg Laying Moon (April)
Tqoljuiku's	Frogs Croaking Moon (May)
Nipniku's	Summer Moon (June)
Peskewiku's	Fur Shedding Moon (July)
Kisaqewiku's	Ripening Moon (August)
Wikumkewiku's	Animal Calling Moon (September)
Wikewiku's	Animals Fat Moon (October)
Keptekewiku's	Ice Film Moon (November)
Punamuiku's	Tom-cod Spawning Moon
Kjiku's/Kesikewiku's	Great* Moon (December)
Apiknajit	Snow Blinding Moon (February)

*The "great" was added after the arrival of Christianity because of the link to the birth of Jesus.

It is natural to wonder where on the Island the ancestors of today's Mi'kmaq camped and lived. The short answer might be "everywhere," but that's not helpful. People are also curious about what the Mi'kmaq ate when they were here and there. That too has a short answer: it depended on the time of year.

A study of ancient Mi'kmaw place names sometimes offers instructive answers to both of those questions. Place names offer clear evidence that people were, there and what they ate when they were there—provided you went at the right time of year, of course, for everything had a cycle. From place names we can often learn why Mi'kmaq traditionally visited certain sites and at what time of year they went there. The place today's Islanders and tourists know as Borden, where the Confederation Bridge touches land, was called Pastue'kati. That meant, "a place where sea cows are plentiful." St. Peters Bay on the north shore was Puku'samkek, which meant "the place where there are plenty of clams in the sand." Savage Harbour on the north shore was Katewpijk, which translates as "eel trap place," one of many place names that refer to eels. The elongated fish were an important part of the ancestors' diet, as they still are for many Mi'kmaq today. Some of the earliest place names recorded by Europeans, such as those that appear on the 1689 map by Pierre Detcheverry (in Chapter 1), are still in use. One well-known example is Malpek, meaning "big bay" or "big body of water." Malpeque Bay today is famous for its oysters. Archaeology has shown us that the rich shellfish and other marine resources of the bay have been sustaining Mi'kmaw communities for millennia.

Aspects of geography are also contained in some of the old names. Darnley, for instance, was called Keji-pukwek. That meant "the place where one is knowledgeable about the many shoals." The name was a warning and a navigational chart all in one!

Place Names Reveal a Lot

The Mi'kmaw place names of Epekwitk are a rich source of information about how the land and its plants and animals were used by ancestral Mi'kmaq. The Mi'kmaq named places for various reasons: as travel routes, landmarks, or gathering places; or as important hunting, fishing, or food-gathering areas. The most numerous are this last type, names that describe where a resource was plentiful. Mi'kmaw place names are rich in good places for eels and eel fishing, areas where bears, sea cows (walrus), and ducks were found, or spots for berries, groundnuts, trout, bass, seals, beech nuts, and clams.

Some of the Mi'kmaq place names of Epekwitk:

Muinewey Sipu ("river of the bear, where the bears are found"): Belle River

Unikansuk ("portage trail"): Clyde River, Portage

Suomane'katik ("the place where beech nuts are plentiful"): Rice Point

Tlaqatik ("the place where people gather"): Tracadie

Representation by artist Francis Back of how a Mi'kmaw family might be dressed and equipped in the early eighteenth century. Courtesy Parks Canada.

In ancient times, the very language of the Mi'kmaq reflected their outlook on the world, as it still does today in those communities and households where it is still spoken. Because languages are not simply collections of words but are the fabric of cultures and express relationships in unique ways, they are windows into how a people thinks. Every language on the planet comes out of a distinctive culture and way of being in the world. When a language slips out of use or is lost, a perspective and way of expressing thoughts and feelings is lost.

The language of the Mi'kmaq has been spoken for millennia, but it has only been written down in one form or another for the past few centuries. It is apparent from the historical record of the early 1600s that the ancestors of today's Mi'kmaq had developed ideograms on their own. These were symbols that stood for certain concepts. Missionary priests in the 1600s and 1700s took those Mi'kmaw ideograms and added some of their own. For the missionaries, the purpose behind such systems of written language was to guide the Mi'kmaq through Christian prayers.

The Lennox Island Micmacs, around 1958. Photo MCPEI Collection.

The Mi'kmaw Language

The overwhelming importance of verbs in the Mi'kmaw language reveals that for the people who developed the language, everything around them was seen as fluid. There was always an idea of potential, and of changing situations or relationships, inherent in the language itself. As for the nouns of the Mi'kmaw language, they are categorized as animate or inanimate. The animate/inanimate distinction suggests that the animate nouns are alive; however, the language suggests that inanimate nouns are simply dormant for the moment, meaning they, too, could change state. Colour, which in English and in French is often categorized as a noun or adjective, is a verb in Mi'kmaw. The Mi'kmaw term that in other languages or other religions might usually be a noun and translate as "the Creator" in Mi'kmaq is "He makes us," a verb phrase that conjugates like any other verb. This suggests that in the Mi'kmaw mind, God is forever changing, just like everything else. A recent study of the Mi'kmaw language, *The Language of the Land, Mi'kma'ki* by Trudy Sable and Bernie Francis, highlights the beauty, complexity, and sophistication of the ancient and still living language.

A Lennox Island baseball team of the 1960s. Front row: Raymond Lewis, Leo Peters, Freddy Scully (bat boy), Albert Bernard, Lawrence Maloney, Moses Bernard. Back row: Alfred Callow, Joe Labobe, Charlie Tuplin, Reuben Tuplin, Lewis Mitchell. Photo courtesy Margaret Labobe.

By 1900 there were two different forms of fully written Mi'kmaw languages, know as the Rand and Pacifique systems, after their authors. Users and champions of each system thought its spelling approach best captured the way in which the language was spoken. Both orthographies used the Roman alphabet, not ideograms as had been used previously. Those Mi'kmaw Elders who grew up with the orthography developed by Father Pacifique in the nineteenth century remain very attached to it. That older spelling approach is still used and taught in some Mi'kmaw areas, especially in Quebec and New Brunswick. Other systems of spelling Mi'kmaw words developed later on. A new orthography, named Smith-Francis after its developers Douglas Smith and Bernie Francis, was introduced in 1974. It has gained steadily in popularity since then. Many Mi'kmaw speakers today, especially on Prince Edward Island and in Nova Scotia, feel it is the closest representation of the way the language is pronounced.

Borrowed Words

The Mi'kmaw language has absorbed certain words from other languages and passed on a few of their own words to others. Basque mariners were among the first Europeans the ancestors encountered, and they took a few words from them. They borrowed even more—over one hundred words—from the French. That's because relations with the French and the Acadians lasted longer and were often close. Here are some examples.

atouray (Pidgin Basque) became *a'tlai* (Mi'kmaq) = shirt
adiu (Basque) and *adieu* (French) became *atiu* (Mi'kmaq) = goodbye
l'assiette (French) became *lassiet* (Mi'kmaq) = plate
la cheminée (French) became *lasimne* (Mi'kmaq) = chimney
petits clous (French) became *pleku* (Mi'kmaq) = one nail
magasin (French) became *makasan* (Mi'kmaq) = store
matelot (French) became *matlot* (Mi'kmaq) = sailor
la moutarde (French) became *lamuta'l* (Mi'kmaq) = mustard
ma poche (French) became *mappos* (Mi'kmaq) = pocket
Sainte-Anne (French) became *Se'tta'n* = St. Anne
Noël (French) became *Nuel* (Mi'kmaq) = Christmas

Acadian historian Régis Brun has found more than sixty words that the Acadians, and sometimes English-speakers, use that came originally from the Mi'kmaw language. Five well-known examples are caribou, moccasin, toboggan, tomahawk, and wigwam.

Young dancers at the Lennox Island Powwow. Photo: Ron Zakar.

The Mitchell Family, Rocky Point, around 1920.
Photo courtesy Vincent Tuplin.

A birthday party, circa 1940. Pictured are Madeline Knockwood, Theresa Lewis, Shirley Feehan and daughter, Emma Francis, Mary Jane Jadis, and Mabel Scully. Photo courtesy family of Linus Peters Collection.

John T. Sark, Lennox Island Chief in the early twentieth century. Photo: A. W. Mitchell, PARO.

David Bernard during his service in World War I. Photo courtesy Cathy Fry.

Good times: a fiddle, a guitar, and a motorcycle. Pictured here are John D. Scully, John Andrew Francis, Rossy Bernard, and Melvin Gallant. Photo courtesy Vincent Tuplin.

Religious celebrations. This unidentified photo is believed to show Lennox Island, circa 1955.

AGNES AUGUSTINE, 1898–1998

Agnes (née Thomas) Augustine was kind and generous. She always seemed to be helping someone out. If she won some money at bingo, chances are the winnings wouldn't go toward a small luxury for her; rather they would quickly end up in the hands of someone she felt required the money more than she did. If someone in need asked Agnes for the loan of some money, Agnes would say she preferred to make it a gift. That was because if the person should be unable to pay her back, Agnes didn't want the money owed to result in the person avoiding her. To Agnes, the money was less important than the person she gave it to.

Agnes and her son Patrick in 1925.
Photo courtesy Stephen Augustine.

Born and raised on Lennox Island to Francis Thomas and Catherine (Bernard) Thomas, Agnes came from a large family that moved extensively, in the traditional Mi'kmaw way. The parents made their living through a wide variety of means, including hunting, fishing, and the manufacture and sale of baskets and crafts.

Agnes met Thomas Théophile Augustine, known as "Basil Tom," when she was thirteen years old. They married a few years later. Basil Tom often worked in the lumber woods. In census records he is listed as a cooper. The couple moved to Big Cove, New Brunswick, in 1924. They had a son and a daughter. Only their son, Patrick Joseph Augustine (Sr.), born in 1924, survived to adulthood.

In 1951, Agnes and Basil Tom moved back to Lennox Island, after his health declined. He passed away in 1956 and is buried on Lennox Island. Agnes also lived subsequently at Scotchfort, Rocky Point, and Vernon Bridge, PEI, this last location to be closer to her brother, John Thomas, and his wife, Mary (Paul) Thomas.

Having grown up largely on the land, Agnes continued throughout her life to nurture a great love of nature and the outdoors. She spent a large amount of time in the woods, so much so that it became a subject people would sometimes tease her about. Her kind and compassionate nature was not limited to people; she was known to frequently feed and look after animals, such as stray dogs.

Agnes Augustine. Photo: MCPEI collection.

Agnes Augustine was a fine basket-maker and could turn her skilled hand to many types of crafts. When picking mayflowers to sell in the spring, for example, she would fashion handsome small baskets from the metal of Carnation milk cans decorated with coloured crêpe paper, to hold the mayflowers.

Even into old age Agnes remained a person of great physical strength and stamina. She was capable of picking one hundred barrels of potatoes in a single day. In a day in the same field, pickers decades younger than her would do well to pick sixty or seventy barrels.

Agnes Augustine, a strong Mi'kmaw woman with a big heart, passed away on December 6, 1998, in Elsipogtog (Big Cove), New Brunswick, at the age of one hundred years.

MR. & MRS. BAZIL T. AUGUSTINE   JUNE 2, 1943
BIG COVE

Agnes and her husband Basil Tom in 1943.
Photo courtesy Stephen Augustine.

"[The Mi'kmaq] love their children much ...
They are never afraid of having too many for
they are their Wealth; the boys aiding their
Father, going on the Hunt & helping in support
of the Family, & the girls aiding their Mother;
going for wood & water & finding the animal
from the Hunt."

—Nicolas Denys, French explorer in Mi'kma'ki, mid-1600s

Woman, Man, and Child

Whether woman, man, or child, every individual in every Mi'kmaw family had a role to play to sustain the family and the community. Women come first in the chapter title because women in Mi'kmaw society are to be especially honoured and respected, and that has long been the case. After all, to give life and do so much to raise children: could there be anything more important than that?

In recent generations, it is most often Mi'kmaw women who possess and pass on to the next generation the knowledge of the ancient medicines. And yet another reason it makes sense to put "woman" first in our title is that the clans of the Mi'kmaq and the family lines of descent have always been based on the woman's side. That makes the Mi'kmaq matrilineal, whereas most European cultures, including England and France, are patrilineal, meaning lineage is traced through the father's side.

Though in traditional times the Mi'kmaq marked descent along the woman's line, their society was matrilineal but not matriarchal. Traditional Mi'kmaw society was patriarchal in the sense that the exercise of power did not lie with women, but with men. Women did not choose the Chiefs (as women did and still do among the Mohawks, for instance). Until fairly recently men occupied most leadership roles in the Island's bands and communities.

Mary Tuplin, Bridget Sark, and Caroline Copage.
Photo courtesy Vincent Tuplin.

Children Come from the Creator

Near the top of the list of surprises for European newcomers when they arrived on these shores was how the Mi'kmaq raised their children. The Europeans were astonished to see how both girls and boys were treated with so much affection and granted so much freedom. The newcomers failed to see that the freedom was not absolute. Everyone in the village kept an eye out for all the children as they came and went. Today, children remain a sacred gift, the Mi'kmaq's greatest pride and joy.

Turning to the last word of the title, the "child," we think it appropriate to present an observation made four hundred years ago. It's from a book written in the mid-1600s by the French explorer and entrepreneur Nicolas Denys. Denys had come from France to what he thought of as Acadie, but which to the Mi'kmaq was but a portion of their traditional territories. Those lands in recent years are collectively called Mi'kma'ki.

Denys spent decades in Atlantic Canada, and though his primary interests were economic—especially the fishery and the fur trade—he was also a keen observer of Mi'kmaw culture and society. He found the ways of the indigenous people of the region offered a fascinating contrast with the customs and thinking of his own people, the seventeenth-century French. The particular passage we present here relates to how the Mi'kmaq raised their children. Denys, like other contemporary Europeans, was struck by how much affection the Mi'kmaq demonstrated for their children.

It was a time when European approaches to raising their young were generally much stricter, sometimes even aloof, compared to what he saw among the Mi'kmaq: "They love their children much.... They are never afraid of having too many for they are their Wealth; the boys aiding their Father, going on the Hunt & helping in support of the Family, & the girls aiding their Mother; going for wood & water & finding the animal from the Hunt."

Though the particular details of Mi'kmaw life have changed greatly from the period Denys describes—with less reliance on hunting and going for wood and water—the deep attachment the Mi'kmaq have for children in their community has not lessened. Babies and young people are prized, encouraged, and celebrated no less now than in Denys's time. These days, such deep-seated affection for children is more universal in Canadian society, but in colonial times it astonished some Europeans that the Mi'kmaq placed so much importance on their children and demonstrated a parenting style Europeans thought was lenient.

At the opposite end of the age spectrum from children come the Elders or "seniors" as they are more generally called in Canada today. The importance of Elders in Mi'kmaw society cannot be overemphasized. They are the keepers of the culture and widely regarded as the wisest and kindest of all.

While all Elders are respected, grandmothers are especially so. The affection for the mother's mother runs deep and wide among the Mi'kmaq. In every community on the Island there are elderly women who are greatly esteemed. It was no accident that in the early 1600s the Christian figure the ancestors of the Mi'kmaq asked missionaries about most was the grandmother of Jesus Christ. It was a natural curiosity based on what they knew in their own communities and their distinctive world view. Christ's grandmother was St. Anne, the mother of the Virgin Mary. It is little surprise that St. Anne was chosen to be the patron saint of the Mi'kmaq. She remains their patron saint, four centuries later.

St. Anne's Day occurs in late July on the church calendar, depending on the year. It's a moveable feast, celebrated the fourth Sunday of July. St. Anne's Day remains for the Mi'kmaq one of the most anticipated and celebrated days of the entire year. While it is a spiritual and religious day, it is also a community gathering, a time for families and entire communities to be together. To mark the occasion as they have for centuries, Mi'kmaq come from far and near to celebrate.

We turn now to the central intimate relationship of the family and the basic unit of society: the relationship between spouses. European explorers were surprised to see how men courted women among the Mi'kmaq. It was nothing like they knew from their home countries. The French explorer Nicolas Denys left behind the following description, written in the mid-1600s:

Martina Tuplin and her husband Vincent Tuplin, when they were living in Presque Isle, Maine, in 1965. Photo courtesy Vincent Tuplin.

In Old Times a boy who wished to have a girl was Obliged to serve her Father for several Years according to an Agreement; going a-hunting to show that he was a good hunter, capable of supporting properly a wife & children…. For her part, the girl corded his snowshoes, made his clothes, his moccasins & his stockings, as evidence that she was Clever in work…. The term being Expired, it was time to speak of the Marriage…. If one of the two wish'd not the Marriage, there was nothing further done; for they were never Compelled into it. But if all were in Agreement, a day was chosen for a Banquet.

Courting may once have looked similar in European societies as well, but not in the time and place in which Denys based his observations. In speaking with Elders, as well as reading accounts left behind by early European writers such as Denys, it is clear that in traditional times—which we leave as a vaguely defined era before about 1800—there was a sharp divide between what was expected of men and women in Mi'kmaw society. The men were hunters and fishers, out in the forest and along many a shore and stream. They were also warriors when enemies had to be beaten back. The women did nearly everything else, which makes for a quite a list. Long and hard the Mi'kmaw women's hours could be, because those hours stretched into days then months and years of preparing meals and medicines.

Some of the many tasks once the exclusive domain of women included butchering, cooking, and preserving meat, including fish. Some of the animals hunted by PEI Mi'kmaq could be huge. Walrus remains are frequently found in PEI archaeological sites; an adult Atlantic walrus weighs on average 908 kg (2,000 lbs).

Then there were the tasks of preparing skins and furs, shaping them into garments and cleaning and decorating them when the clothes were made. Next, there were containers to be made, arrows to be fletched, wigwams to be erected, canoes to be caulked, the carrying of everything when a seasonal move had to be made, and more. Picking berries, making dyes, cording snowshoes, making or repairing nets, and, of course, looking after children.

Detail, quillwork basket, from the collection of the Prince Edward Island Museum and Heritage Foundation. Photo by John Sylvester, copyright Mi'kmaq Confederacy of PEI.

Women's Work 500 Years Ago

Archaeology sometimes sheds light on gender roles. The archaeological excavation depicted in the image above took place in 1987–88 at Robinsons Island (Rustico Island) on the north shore, in Prince Edward Island National Park. Birgitta Wallace of Parks Canada led the project. The dig uncovered shell middens. These middens are left behind where the edible parts of shellfish are processed. The shells left behind were well-preserved in the Island's soil. In ancient days, according to the oral traditions that have come down to us, processing shellfish was work for women and children. The older boys and men, on the other hand, were hunters and fishers. Beneath the midden was an older campsite that dated back to between 500 and 1,500 years ago, during a time archaeologists call the Middle Woodland or Ceramic period and called in Mi'kmaq the time of "recent people" (*Kejikwe'k L'nu'k*). One site on top of another suggests a continuous use of the area. Bones of bear, walrus, and mink were also found on the site, which means the spot was used for hunting during different seasons, as well as the harvest of shellfish in the summer.

Sally Mitchell, Rocky Point, circa 1895–1905. Photo: A.W. Mitchell, courtesy PARO.

Robinsons Island archaeological excavation led by Birgitta Wallace, Parks Canada, 1988. Image courtesy Parks Canada.

Charlotte Town taken from J.S. McGill farm, 1836, by George Thresher. Courtesy PARO.

In today's world, the girls and boys of the Mi'kmaq are more equal and are free to find whatever role in life and work that suits them best.

To close this chapter we offer this story by Alma MacDougall of the Abegweit First Nation. Alma uses the birch tree as a metaphor for the hardships and struggles, but also for the resiliency, of Mi'kmaw individuals and communities.

"The Birch People", by Alma MacDougall

This story is an inspiration from the spirits of our Mi'kmaq Ancestors; it came on a bright sunny, winter day when the snow glistened like shimmering diamond, blanket across the land in which we live. As you all know, many of the strong, hardy canoes, baskets and utensils were made by our ancestors in birch to assist them with their daily lives. Hear me now as I tell a little story.

It is a story of our relatives the Birch Tree People. Have you ever been out on a cold stormy, cold winter's day? Look at the Birch Family; the mothers, the fathers, the children, the brothers and sisters are all affected by the harshness of the winter. Some are straight and tall while others bend with the weight of ice and snow. Occasionally and only occasionally, you see that one of the Birch Families is bent and broken.

But as the spring and warmth approaches, the mighty Birch Family resumes its straightness and once again reaches for the sky. The weight of the world has been lifted from their sturdy, tall, proud backs. The others who have broken slowly wither away to death or start to regain some of shoots and begin slowly begin its long journey back to life.

The Birch Tree people love and support their fellow trees, but is powerless to stop the abuse nature has given its brothers or sisters and children. All they can do is hope and pray that at the end of that long, cold winter, their children, brothers and sisters can cope until they are returned to their loving warm embrace. The ones who have died are the ones who could no longer bear the weight of nature's wrath. It was not through any weakness that birch tree had broken or died, it had but only the weight, the neglect and the sorrows it felt during this trying time.

This is where the lessons from the Birch Tree Family come to the Mi'kmaq People who have had to endure the Indian Residential School system. Once a tall, sturdy and proud people, the Survivors have had to endure that winter- like times while away at Shubenacadie Residential School.

The Birch Tree (*Maskwi*)

Long ago, back when the ancestors of today's Mi'kmaq moved according to the seasons, the white birch was of great importance. Its bark was durable, light, and waterproof, so it was ideal for covering wigwams and canoes and also for making cups, bowls, and pots. Summer bark, the most easily detached, was harvested in July or August, when the fireflies appear. Winter bark was harvested when it was really cold. The bark is denser then and it must be heated gently over coals, rolling the log, in order to get it detached as a sheet. It was the winter bark that was used for canoes. A whole tree is required to obtain enough bark for a continuous, single row of a wigwam's construction.

A great many of the Survivors have returned home tall, straight and proud but carry the scars left by the damage done to them during those dark days. A few of those who bent to the point of breaking carry deep scars of those dark winters, but now have those tender shoots of life and the long journey of re-growth. Those who had crossed over to live with the Ancestors did so only as a result of neglect, abuse and illness. Not of their own choosing or perhaps as a result of the Creator's mercy.

Here is where the Residential School Survivors receive their strength to carry on; it comes from our relatives the Birch Trees and the Ancestors. *Msit No'kmaq*

Mi'kmaw Veterans

Young Mi'kmaq have many role models to inspire them, coming from many walks of life. Heroes remembered with special pride are the many Mi'kmaw veterans. Their story is one that everyone—Mi'kmaq or not—should know.

When World War I broke out, Island Mi'kmaq responded to the call to arms like no other group. The Mi'kmaw community provided more recruits per capita than any other group across Prince Edward Island. From Lennox Island, thirty-two of sixty-four eligible men, half of the adult population, enlisted to go overseas. Seven were killed in action, while thirteen more were wounded. In World War II, thirty-four of Prince Edward Island's Mi'kmaq enlisted for military service. Seven joined up for the Korean War (1950–53). Despite this ultimate act of citizenship, it was not until 1956 that "Indians" as defined by the "Indian Act" were recognized as citizens of Canada. And it was not until 1960 that all restrictions were lifted on Aboriginal people being allowed to vote in federal elections.

Dan Mitchell, boy soldier. In 1916, at the age of fourteen years, Dan Mitchell ran away from home to enlist in the army and fight in World War I. When his parents discovered what he had done, they sent Dan's uncle, Jacob Sark, to make his way to Moncton to get Dan to return home. Dan had already succeeded in enlisting, and he was so proud of his uniform that his uncle didn't have the heart to make him come home. Photo MCPEI Collection / John Joe Sark.

One of PEI's many Mi'kmaw veterans, Daniel Bernard, veteran of both World Wars. Photo courtesy Albert Bernard.

Jacob Peters (1897–1922), a World War I veteran from Lennox Island, fought with the 105th infantry battalion — the PEI Highlanders. Photo courtesy Mi'kmaq Confederacy of PEI Collection.

MATILDA LEWIS, 1902–1994

Visitors were often to be found in the kitchen of Matilda (Knockwood) Lewis. Though they might have enjoyed the tea or the *Luskinikin* (similar to bannock) and molasses, what they really came for was Matilda's love of people, her personal warmth, her enjoyment of a good laugh, her knack for telling a good story, and her delight in lively conversation, especially in the Mi'kmaw language. It was that warmth that earned Matilda the name *"Giju"* or "Mum" among not just her family but her entire community.

Matilda Lewis. Photo: Lionel Stevenson.

Born on Lennox Island, Matilda grew up primarily speaking the Mi'kmaw language, and for the rest of her life, it was the language in which she was most at ease. Likewise, from her childhood, the Catholic faith and worship at St. Anne's Church remained deeply important to her. That faith found voice through prayer and annual pilgrimages to Ste. Anne de Beaupré Cathedral outside Quebec City.

Matilda married Denny Lewis on May 27, 1919, and their marriage was a loving and devoted one for the next fifty-four years, until Denny's death in 1973. Together, they had six children, three of whom survived to adulthood. Denny served in both World Wars, and for much of his life, he was bothered by skin problems resulting from exposure to mustard gas in World War I. Like many Mi'kmaq, Denny and Matilda lived in Boston for several years before returning home to Lennox Island.

Matilda and Denny supported their household through a mix of farming, hunting, fishing, and the sale of baskets and crafts. Many examples of her fine baskets remain cherished possessions of collectors and family members.

She had such a gregarious personality and long life, many recall stories about Matilda. One story comes from Bessie MacNeill, who ran a store with her husband for many decades in neighbouring Tyne Valley. She remembered how Matilda and Denny would walk across the ice to trade their crafts for provisions at MacNeill's store. Over the years, Matilda taught Bessie some Mi'kmaw greetings and the Mi'kmaw alphabet.

Nearly two decades after her passing, many Island Mi'kmaq fondly remember *Giju* as a woman at the heart of her family and her community life.

Baskets by Matilda "*Giju*" Lewis, from the Ray Sark Collection of Mi'kmaw Baskets. Photo: John Sylvester, courtesy John Sylvester, Ron Walsh, and Fran Sark.

Matilda Lewis making a basket.

Acknowledgements

The authors would like to acknowledge and respectfully thank the groups and individuals named below for the advice and assistance they provided to turn an idea into a book.

We are grateful to the following groups and organizations:

The many Mi'kmaw Elders who shared their stories and perspectives with us over the past several decades.

The Mi'kmaq Confederacy of PEI for its encouragement and support.

Parks Canada for the use of numerous images and for assistance in many ways.

Family members who assisted with biographies: Stephen Augustine, Jean Tuplin, Roseanne Sark, Chief Matilda Ramjattan, Lillian Haroulakis, and Angela Haroulakis.

The many people who allowed the MCPEI to use family and personal photographs. Their generosity has helped to make this book more engaging and interesting. Special mention goes to Vincent Tuplin and Margaret Labobe who generously shared many photos.

Members of the Advisory Committee: Judy Clark, Darrell Desroches, Helen Kristmanson, Barb MacDonald, Tiffany Sark, Tammy MacDonald, and Sandra Gaudet, who provided valuable suggestions and guidance to the travelling exhibition and to this book.

And we thank these individuals (in alphabetical order):

Andre Bilodeau at Design Plus Communications for providing scans from his files.

Former Chief Darlene Bernard for her support of this project.

Stéphane Breton for combining texts and images into a design that the authors greatly admire, just as they were impressed by the design he did on the exhibition of the same name.

Terrilee Bulger of The Acorn Press for supporting the concept for this book right from the start.

J.P. and Sally Camus, with whom the authors of this book worked so closely on the exhibition of the same name, and who in countless ways helped this book along.

Judy Clark, who helped in many ways, including involving Elders and community members and helping gather photos.

Dr. Bernie Francis for translations into the Mi'kmaw language.

Sandra Gaudet for her excellent guidance.

Karen Jans for her support.

Evelyn Joe for allowing us to use the poems by her mother, Rita Joe.

David Keenlyside and The PEI Museum and Heritage Foundation for permission and assistance in allowing us to photograph objects from the collection.

Helen Kristmanson for her contributions and particular help with archaeology-related questions.

Jane Ledwell for providing much appreciated editorial advice and suggestions.

Tammy MacDonald for her assistance with research.

Alma MacDougall for allowing us to use her story about "The Birch Tree People."

Julie Pellisier-Lush for generous assistance with photographs and captions.

Vienna Sanipass and Metepenagiag Heritage Park for permission to reproduce the paintings of Roger Simon.

Keptin John Joe Sark for allowing us to use a version of the Kluskap legend that he had published previously and for permission to reproduce the painting by Michael Francis.

Lionel Stevenson for permission to use his photo of Matilda Lewis.

John Sylvester for his excellent contributions to this book.

John Sylvester, Ron Walsh, and Fran Sark for allowing us to use photos from the catalogue of The Ray Sark Collection of Mi'kmaw Baskets.

Ruth Holmes Whitehead for her detailed and extremely helpful suggestions.

Many of the motifs used in the design of this book are from Nova Scotia Mi'kmaw petroglyphs. Courtesy Nova Scotia Museum and Parks Canada.